# SNAKES
## OF THE
# WORLD

# SNAKES
## OF THE
# WORLD

Chris Mattison

BLANDFORD

Paperback edition first published in the UK 1992
by Blandford, a Cassell imprint

Cassell plc,
Wellington House
125 Strand
London
WC2R OBB

Reprinted 1995 & 1998

Previously published in hardback by Blandford in 1986
Reprinted 1988, 1989, 1990, & 1992

Distributed in the United States by
Sterling Publishing Co., Inc.,
387 Park Avenue South, New York, NY 10016-8810


A Cataloguing-in-Publication Data entry for this title is available
from the British Library

ISBN 0-7137-2340-8


Typeset in Hong Kong by Graphicraft Typesetters Ltd

Printed and bound by Colorcraft Ltd, Hong Kong

# Contents

To my children, Vicky and James

# Acknowledgements

Although I am a firm believer in taking pictures of wild animals in their natural surroundings, this was not always possible when compiling the photographs which were necessary to illustrate this book, and I have had to rely heavily on the generosity of various people and institutions who have allowed me to use animals in their collections, or who have obtained specimens for me. In this respect I am pleased to acknowledge the help of the following: Chester Zoo (Isolde MacGeorge and Keith Brown); Cotswold Wildlife Park (Don Reid); Knaresborough Zoo (Nick Nyoka); Dennis Lee; Mark O'Shea; Jim Pether; John Pickett; Poole Aquarium (Gary Lilley); Phil Reid; James Savage; Sheffield Polytechnic (Sandra Britten); Arthur Stevenson; Twycross Zoo (Chris Howard); and Xotic Pets Ltd of Alfreton. Special thanks are due to Mike Nolan, not only for providing snakes for several of the plates, but also for his help in photographing the *Cerastes* fangs.

Plate 74 was supplied by Ellen Marsden, Plates 51 and 58 by Bill Montgomery, and Plate 3 by Morley Read. Figures 9, 11 and 12 were drawn by Isabelle Naylor and Figures 4, 5, 6 and 13 by Don Reid. Josie Healey and Anne Brennan typed the manuscript. To all of these people, many thanks!

My long-suffering wife and children accompanied me on many trips to southern Europe in order to gather material, and in Trinidad I was fortunate to be helped by Robin Mattison, Bill Montgomery and Dave Reznick, all of whom provided humour as well as practical assistance.

Finally, I must acknowledge the encouragement given by a number of people, but especially by the editors of Blandford Press and my parents, without whose moral support the book would never have been completed.

# Introduction

At an early age I came to the conclusion that those organisms which are universally feared and loathed are invariably the most interesting. This opinion has not been modified over the years and I still find pleasure in studying such creatures as leeches, bats, spiders, scorpions and, most of all, reptiles. I saw my first wild snake on a heath near Bournemouth, England, when I was about ten years old. It was an adder, and I caught it by the tail and a friend took a photograph of the two of us. The photograph has long since been lost, but my fascination for snakes grew to obsessive proportions, much to the consternation of parents, friends and, later on, employers. What is it about snakes which attracts some people and repels others? I can only talk about the attraction, for, though I respect the ability of some species to cause a rapid and somewhat sensational death, outright fear of them is, to me, irrational.

Like most species of animals, snakes kill for only two reasons – hunger or fear. To be close to a dangerous species is a unique and awe-inspiring experience. Their supreme arrogance, developed over millions of years as masters of their environment, commands respect out of all proportion to their size. Even harmless kinds make the heart beat faster when they hiss and strike at their tormentor, or when they glide away without appearing to move and are suddenly gone.

If you look closely at their skin you will see scales arranged with geometrical precision, forming a mosaic of colours and patterns which gives each species its identity. Snakes are not only beautiful in appearance but also mysterious in habits. These two qualities provide the perfect combination for those of us with an inquiring mind and a strong hunting instinct. My own hunting is strictly for pleasure, the trophy being a photograph or, very occasionally, a specimen living in a close simulation of its natural habitat to remind me of privileged moments. I can gaze at many of the photographs in this book and be transported back to some of the most thrilling experiences of my life – the sand viper, exposed to view suddenly by turning a rock, a rock which was like about two thousand others I had turned that day on the Greek island of Naxos; the ladder snake, uncovered accidentally by my wife, in the middle of a car park in a Spanish mountain range, after I had spent all day looking vainly in the snakiest places imaginable; and, perhaps most of all, the bushmaster, sprawled across a jungle road one rainy night in Trinidad.

It is this unexpectedness of snakes which is so fascinating. Finding a snake is like finding the needle in a haystack, where the haystack is a boulder-strewn hillside, an acre of reed-bed, or 100 square miles of tropical rainforest.

There is also something else about snakes. Observe the people in the reptile house at a zoo – the lizards may be prettier, the frogs more active, and the turtles more amusing, but it is the snakes which draw the crowds. How? By just sitting there and *being* snakes. Why is there this fascination for long shiny animals with no legs and a flickering tongue? Who knows? Whatever the reasons, snakes are amongst the most hated, most worshipped, and least known animals sharing our planet. This book will, I hope, help to shed some of the mystery about snakes without detracting from the wonderment that they arouse.

*Chapter 1*

# What are Snakes?

Snakes are members of the class Reptilia – the reptiles. More precisely, they form part of the order Squamata, which also includes the closely related lizards (about 3,000 species) and amphisbaenians (about 140 species). The snakes, of which there are approximately 2,700 species, comprise the sub-order Serpentes (sometimes known as Ophidia).

The other orders of reptiles are the Testudines (turtles and tortoises – about 230 species), the Crocodilia (crocodiles and alligators – 21 species) and the Rhynchocephalia (tuatara – 1 species).

All of these animals are characterised by having a scaly skin which helps to protect them from desiccation in dry environments, an advantage which historically enabled them to move out over the land, breaking the tie with water which still limits the distribution of their ancestors, the amphibians. Also important in this respect is their ability to produce a shelled egg (or, in some cases, living young) within which the embryo can develop in a suitable micro-environment, thus avoiding the necessity to return to the water in order to breed. (Rather perversely, some reptiles which went back to an aquatic way of life, for instance turtles, now have to leave the water and return temporarily to the land to breed.)

The snakes are the most recently evolved group of reptiles, probably having first appeared during the early Cretaceous period 120 million years ago. This was towards the end of the Mesozoic era – the 'Age of the Reptiles'. Although fossil records of them are rather thin on the ground, it is generally believed that they arose from a line of lizards or lizard-like animals which adopted a subterranean life-style. In order to burrow more effectively these animals lost their limbs (as several modern burrowing lizards have done) and grew a transparent covering, the brille, to protect their eyes in place of movable eyelids. In time, the limb-girdles degenerated and the external ear-drum, or tympanum, was lost (although the main components of the ear are still present internally).

Since their appearance, snakes have adapted to most types of habitat found in the world, their only serious limitation being the inability to produce heat internally, forcing them to rely on external sources in order to raise their body temperature to a level necessary for them to function properly (somewhere around 25–30°C, 77–86°F, depending on species). For this reason, snakes are most numerous, both in terms of individuals and of species, in tropical regions, with their numbers falling off as the

Plate 1    The adder, *Vipera berus*, occurs up to 68°N – further north than any other snake.

poles are approached, the most northerly species being the adder, *Vipera berus* (Plate 1), and the common garter snake, *Thamnophis sirtalis*, reaching 68°N and 67°N in Scandinavia and North America respectively, whereas in the south a pit viper, *Bothrops ammodytoides*, occurs to approximately 45°S in Argentina. Altitude also affects temperature and the highest recorded species is *Agkistrodon himalayanus*, which ranges up to 4,900 m (16,000 ft) in the Himalayas.

Animals which cannot produce their own body-heat are known as ectotherms, as opposed to those which can (birds and mammals) which are known as endotherms. Snakes may be loosely defined, therefore, as ectothermic vertebrates with elongated bodies covered in scales, and having no limbs or limb-girdles (except the most primitive families, which retain traces of the pelvic girdle and hind-limbs), no external ear-openings, and no movable eyelids. Internally, their organs are necessarily elongated and the left lung may be absent altogether or very much smaller than the right. They usually have a single row of wide scales beneath the body, each corresponding to a vertebra and a pair of ribs, and all have a long, forked tongue.

Plate 2   The slow-worm, *Anguis fragilis*, is a legless lizard and can be distinguished from snakes by the presence of eyelids.

It is worth pointing out that legless lizards occur in several families, for instance in the Anguidae (slow-worm, glass lizards), the Scincidae (skinks), and the Pygopodidae (snake-lizards), and that some of these also

**Table 1:   Morphological Differences between Snakes and Lizards**

|  | *Snakes* | *Lizards* |
|---|---|---|
| Front limbs | Never | Usually |
| Front limb-girdles | Never | Always |
| Hind limbs | Rarely (vestigial) | Usually |
| Hind limb-girdles | Rarely | Always |
| Single row of ventral scales | Usually | Never |
| Moveable eyelids | Never | Usually |
| External ear-drums | Never | Usually |
| Deeply forked tongue | Usually | Rarely |

Plate 3 *Amphisbaena alba*, a large South American amphisbaenid. Note the segmented body which gives these animals their common name of 'worm lizard', although they are neither worms nor lizards.

share other snake-like characteristics (Plates 2–3). None, however, satisfy all of the criteria listed in Table 1.

## Nomenclature

It is not possible to study a group of animals seriously without using an accepted system of labelling each species, thereby avoiding confusion by researchers who may be working independently in different parts of the world or at different times.

Whenever a new species is discovered it is described in detail in a scientific journal and is given two (or sometimes three) latinised names. The first is the name of the 'genus' into which the animal is placed and tells us that it is closely related to other animals already placed in that genus. If it is not closely related to any known species a new genus is created. This name is written in italics and begins with a capital letter, and is known as the 'generic' name.

The second is the name given to that particular 'species' and is therefore different from the name of any other animal in the same genus.

(A species is a population, or group of populations, of animals which can interbreed to produce fertile offspring.) This second name is also written in italics but does not begin with a capital letter. It is known as the 'specific' name.

If several populations of a species are found which are obviously distinct, but which can still interbreed, these may be known as 'subspecies', in which case animals from each population will be given a third name, also written in italics and without a capital, and known as the 'subspecific' name. The population from which the original specimen was described will have the specific name repeated, and is known as the 'nominate' subspecies.

Each subsequent name therefore tells us a little more about the precise identity of the animal being referred to. If only the generic and specific names are given this indicates that either no subspecies are recognised or that all forms of the species are included. For example, the genus *Elaphe* contains a number of species of harmless constrictors found in North America, Europe and Asia. One of these is *Elaphe obsoleta*, the ratsnake of eastern North America, and this species occurs in several geographical variants, each having different colours and markings, the nominate one being *Elaphe obsoleta obsoleta*, the black ratsnake. Some of the other subspecies are *Elaphe obsoleta quadrivittata*, the yellow ratsnake, *Elaphe obsoleta lindheimeri*, the Texas ratsnake, and *Elaphe obsoleta spiloides*, the grey ratsnake. (Note that latinised names are often abbreviated where there is no possibility of confusion. Thus, in the above example, the subspecies may have been written *Elaphe o. obsoleta*, *Elaphe o. lindheimeri* etc, or even *E. o. obsoleta* if the genus and species had been mentioned previously in the same paragraph.)

The latinised name may be descriptive, e.g. '*quadrivittata*' (= four stripes); it may refer to the place of collection, e.g. '*californiae*' (= of California); or it may commemorate the original collector or an eminent researcher in the appropriate field of herpetology, e.g. '*klauberi*' (after Laurence Klauber, who did much important work on rattlesnakes). On the other hand, the meaning of some names may be obscure, especially if they were described many years ago, and they may even be downright misleading, e.g. '*getulus*', as in *Lampropeltis getulus*, alludes to a region of North Africa – this species, however (a kingsnake), occurs only in North America!

Unfortunately, as our knowledge of the relationships between species increases, animals sometimes need to be moved from one genus to another, leading to a change in their generic names (but not their specific names), or it may be that two examples of the same species are described independently and given separate names (homonyms), in which case the name which was published first has priority. On the other hand, some species, originally described as one, are later found to consist of two or more species with similar appearance, in which case new names must be found. However, these are exceptional cases, and most scientific names are relatively stable and can be relied upon.

Genera which are closely related and which are therefore assumed to have arisen from a common ancestor are grouped together in a 'family'. The family name begins with a capital letter and always ends in '-idae', but is not printed in italics and does not form part of the latinised name. Families may be divided into sub-families (ending in '-inae'), and a number of families form an order or sub-order (as with snakes). Thus, going back to our previous example, *Elaphe obsoleta quadrivittata* belongs to the family Colubridae, which is part of the sub-order Serpentes of the order Squamata:

Class: Reptilia
Order: Squamata
  Sub-order: Serpentes
Family: Colubridae
  Sub-family: Colubrinae
Genus: *Elaphe*
Species: *obsoleta*
Subspecies: *quadrivittata*

The Burmese python, *Python molurus bivittatus*, gives us another example:

Class: Reptilia
Order: Squamata
  Sub-order: Serpentes
Family: Boidae
  Sub-family: Pythoninae
Genus: *Python*
Species: *molurus*
Subspecies: *bivittatus*

The most important divisions here are class, order, family, genus and species.

At present, 11 families of snakes are recognised and although they will be dealt with systematically in Chapter 9 it is worth introducing them at this point (see Table 2) so that reference can be made to some of them in the thematic accounts which follow.

## Table 2:  Snake Families and Number of Species

| Family | Approximate number of species |
|---|---|
| Leptotyphlopidae (thread snakes) | 50 |
| Typhlopidae (blind snakes) | 180 |
| Anomalepidae | 20 |
| Uropeltidae (shield-tailed snakes) | 40 |
| Aniliidae (pipe snakes) | 10 |
| Xenopeltidae (sunbeam snake) | 1 |
| Boidae (boas and pythons) | 95 |
| Acrochordidae (wart snakes) | 3 |
| Colubridae ('typical' snakes) | 2200 |
| Elapidae (cobras etc) | 169 |
| Viperidae (vipers and pit vipers) | 182 |

# Chapter 2

# Size, Shape and Function

Compared with most animals, the snakes have achieved a high level of design economy. They have no limbs, crests, frills, flaps or other adornments and consist basically of three parts – a head, a body and a tail. The head and neck region is only slightly distinct from the body in terms of diameter. The body itself, comprising the largest portion of the animal, is roughly cylindrical in shape but slightly flattened on the undersurface, and there may be a slight ridge on each side where this joins the flanks. The vent, or cloaca, which is the common opening for excretory and reproductive systems, marks the end of the body and the beginning of the tail, which tapers gradually to a fairly sharp point.

This description, which applies to the vast majority of species (**Plate 4**),

Plate 4   The horseshoe snake, *Coluber hippocrepis*, a typical, medium-sized snake from southern Spain and North Africa.

represents what could be thought of as the 'standard model'. What then are the features which enable us to tell one kind from the 2,700-odd others? To establish this we need to look a little more closely. The colours and arrangements of the markings are obviously important, and they will be dealt with in Chapter 3. Size and shape will be dealt with here, together with the various other external features which combine to give each species its individuality. Structural modifications, mostly associated with specialised life-styles, will also be discussed.

## Size

Snakes range in size from 10 mm ($4\frac{1}{2}$ in) to 10 m (32 ft). The longest recorded specimen was a reticulated python, *Python reticulatus*, which is a common species from South-east Asia. However, this is quite a slender species, and the heaviest snake would undoubtedly be the South American anaconda, *Eunectes murinus*, with a maximum recorded length of around 9 m (30 ft) and a probable weight in excess of 150 kg (330 lb). The matter is further complicated by the fact that the latter species ranges over a large area which is relatively unexplored and difficult to penetrate, leading one to predict that larger examples are awaiting discovery. Most of the other 'giants' belong to the same family as the reticulated python and anaconda (the Boidae), and include the African python, *P. sebae* – to 9 m (30 ft); the amethystine python, *P. amethystinus*, from Australia – to 7 m (23 ft); the Indian python, *P. molurus* – to 6.5 m (21 ft); and the Central and South American boa, *Boa constrictor* – to 6 m (20 ft). As may be expected, many exaggerated claims of record anacondas and pythons have been put forward – some of these can be explained by the difficulty in estimating the length of snakes when seen amongst undergrowth; others are simply tall stories.

Large species from other families include the king cobra, *Ophiophagus hannah* – to 4.8 m (16 ft); the black mamba, *Dendroaspis polylepis* – to 4.3 m (14 ft) (Elapidae); the bushmaster, *Lachesis muta* – to 3 m (10 ft) (Viperidae); and the Indian ratsnake, *Ptyas mucosus* – to 3.5 m (11 ft) (Colubridae).

The longest North American snakes are: indigo snake, *Drymarchon corais* – to 2.6 m ($8\frac{1}{2}$ ft); eastern coachwhip, *Masticophis flagellum* – to 2.6 m ($8\frac{1}{2}$ ft); black ratsnake, *Elaphe obsoleta* – to 2.6 m ($8\frac{1}{2}$ ft); and the eastern diamondback rattlesnake, *Crotalus adamanteus* – to 2.4 m (8 ft). In Europe a whipsnake, *Coluber jugularis*, reaches 3 m (10 ft), and the four-lined snake, *Elaphe quatuorlineata*, a more heavily-built animal, 2.5 m ($8\frac{1}{4}$ ft).

These record sizes are not typical for their species, however, and presumably represent individuals which have been unusually successful in finding food and which have outlived their contemporaries and continued to grow, albeit slowly, to an abnormally large size.

The dubious honour of being the smallest snake is said to belong to a thread snake, *Leptotyphlops bilineata*, from the West Indies, although several other members of its family, and also of the Typhlopidae (worm snakes) are also very small and, since so few are collected, it is quite possible that others are even smaller than this one.

All of the examples cited above, of course, are extremes. The vast majority of snakes fall within the range 45–200 cm (18–78 in) in total length, of which 10–20 per cent is tail.

## Scales

Snakes are completely covered in scales (Plate 5). Unlike the scales of fish, which are attached to the skin, snake scales are part of it, formed from localised thickened areas. They serve to prevent desiccation, to take the wear and tear associated with friction, and help in locomotion. Different areas of the snake's body are covered by different types of scales: those on the head which, in most species, are large and of irregular shape (Plates 6–8); those on the dorsal surface, which are smaller, roughly diamond-shaped and overlapping; and those on the ventral surface which are normally wide and arranged as a single row from chin to vent, and single *or* paired beneath the tail, depending on species.

Plate 5   Snake scales are formed from thickened parts of the skin, shown here from the 'inside' of a section of skin from a water snake, *Nerodia*.

The number, shape and arrangement of scales tend to be fairly constant within a given species and are therefore much used as an aid to identification, the critical points being the arrangement of those on the head, the number of dorsal scale-rows at mid-body, and the number of ventral and sub-caudal scales. The latter values differ between the sexes, and males, which have longer tails, usually possess a greater number of sub-caudal scales than their female counterparts. The arrangement and nomenclature of head and body scales is shown in Figs. 1–3.

The dorsal scales may be smooth, keeled or granular, according to

Fig. 1 Nomenclature of the scales on the head of a typical snake (Colubridae). Variation in the number and arrangement of these helps to differentiate each species.

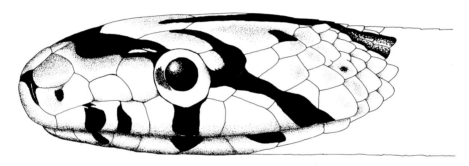

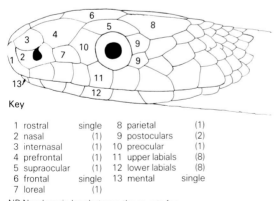

Key

| 1 rostral | single | 8 parietal | (1) |
|-----------|--------|------------|-----|
| 2 nasal | (1) | 9 postoculars | (2) |
| 3 internasal | (1) | 10 preocular | (1) |
| 4 prefrontal | (1) | 11 upper labials | (8) |
| 5 supraocular | (1) | 12 lower labials | (8) |
| 6 frontal | single | 13 mental | single |
| 7 loreal | (1) | | |

NB Numbers in brackets are the counts for the various scales for this example. These counts refer to number per side, but certain scales are centrally placed and are therefore invariably single.

Plate 6    The heads of typical snakes are covered with large scales: *Nerodia cyclopion*.

Plate 7    The heads of boas and pythons are covered with numerous small scales: *Candoia aspera*, the Pacific ground boa.

Plate 8    Vipers, such as this rattlesnake, *Crotalus atrox*, also have small scales on their heads.

Plate 9    Smooth glossy scales: indigo snake, *Drymarchon corais*.

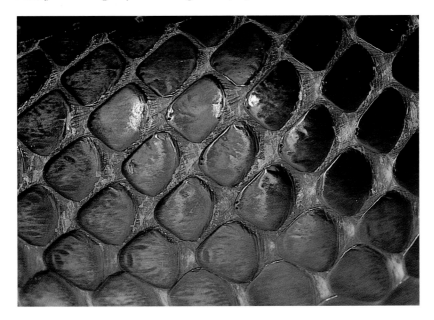

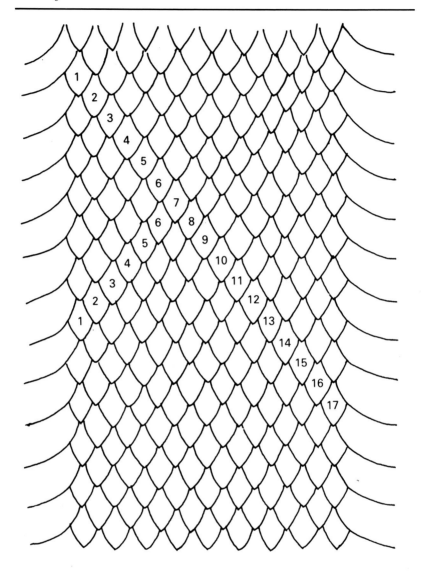

Fig. 2   Arrangement of the dorsal scales, showing two methods of counting the rows.

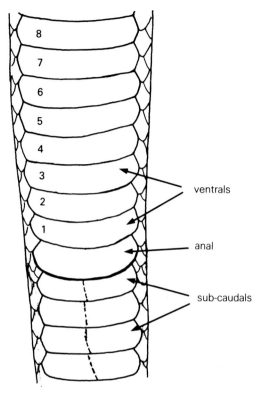

Fig. 3    Arrangement of the ventral and sub-caudal scales. The anal scale may be divided or entire, as may the sub-caudals.

species (Plates 9–11), and in most species each possesses a pair of apical pits, small, circular areas where the scale is thin, and these appear to function as heat-sensing zones. Similar areas are also found in clusters on the scales of the head, and certain scales on the chin and throat, and occasionally also in the vent region, have small tubercles on them which are sensitive to touch, and these appear to play a role in the stimulation of courting snakes.

A number of species, belonging to at least two families, have rough, heavily-keeled scales on their flanks which can be rubbed together when the snake is coiled to produce a harsh, rasping sound if the snake is molested. It has been proposed that one of these species, the African egg-eating snake, *Dasypeltis scabra*, behaves in this manner to mimic a highly venomous viper, *Cerastes cerastes*, which is well-known for such displays.

25

Plate 10    Rough keeled scales: gaboon viper, *Bitis gabonica*.

Plate 11    Granular scales, found in only one family, the Acrochordidae (wart snakes).

26

## Locomotion

Snakes make use of various groups of scales when moving. For instance, when progressing in a straight line (rectilinear locomotion), the snake uses its ventral scales by moving them forward in a continuous series of waves and hitching their edges over irregularities, then using this grip it pulls itself along by muscular effort. At any given time, several adjacent scales will be moving forward, while others will be pulling, so the general impression is of a smooth, gliding motion (Fig. 4). The giant snakes, pythons and boas, use this method of locomotion almost exclusively when they reach a large size. In climbing, snakes use their ventral scales in a slightly different way – here they provide an anchor for the lower part of the body and the tail as they reach forward with the head and neck. When the scales in this region have obtained a grip, the rest of the body and tail are drawn up and the process starts again. It is interesting to note that a number of unrelated snakes which are aquatic and therefore have no use for this type of locomotion have ventral scales which are reduced in size or absent altogether. These species include all three members of the wart snake family, Acrochordidae, the bizarre fishing snake, *Erpeton tentaculatum*, and most of the sea snakes, sub-family Hydrophinae.

The dorsal scales, especially those on the lower flanks, help to propel the snake along when it is moving in the more usual 'serpentine' manner. These scales gain purchase against small irregularities in the substrate, and by movements of the muscles connecting the skin to the ribs the animal thrusts its body forward (Fig. 5). One peculiarity of this form of locomotion is that the whole of the snake's body and tail follows the same course as its head – neither takes any 'short cuts' and each group of muscles pushes against the same points of contact as those which went before it. Returning to our aquatic species, exactly the same form of locomotion serves to propel these species, the sides of the animal thrusting against the water instead of a solid object in order to achieve the same result.

Finally, a rather specialised form of locomotion makes use of the ventral scales *and* those on the flanks. This is sidewinding (Fig. 6), favoured by snakes living on the unstable substrate found in deserts etc. These species travel at an angle of about 45° to the approximate line of their body. They raise their head and 'throw' it forward in the direction of travel, and as it makes contact with the ground a loop of body follows it. By the time half of the body has been moved, the head is raised for the next step and so the

Fig. 4   In rectilinear locomotion, the snake moves in a straight line.

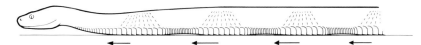

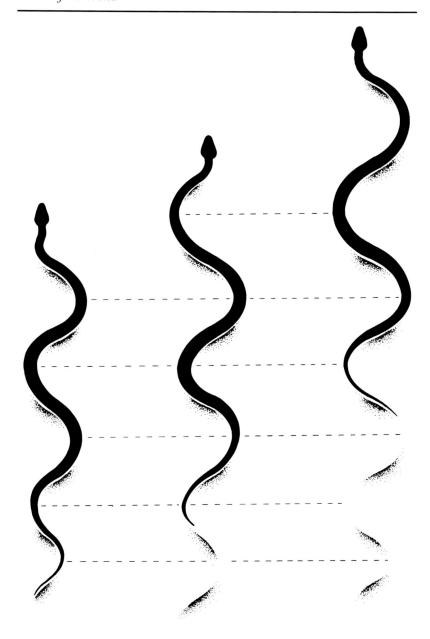

Fig. 5   Typical serpentine locomotion relies on the resistance of irregularities in the surface to provide anchor points. The same movements are made when swimming, when the water is used to provide thrust.

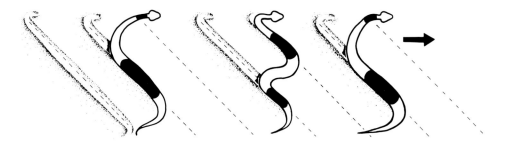

Fig. 6   Sidewinding involves 'throwing' the head and body forward at an angle to the direction of travel.

process continues, leaving a trail of characteristic 'J'-shaped markings across the sand. The main proponents of this unconventional mode of travel are specialised desert species from several widely separated parts of the world: the American sidewinder, *Crotalus cerastes* (a small rattlesnake); the horned viper, *Cerastes cerastes*, and the carpet viper, *Echis carinatus*, from North Africa and the Middle East; and *Bitis peringueyi*, another small viper, this time from South Africa. However, many, if not most, other species of snakes will sidewind to some extent if faced with a loose, powdery substrate and, conversely, all true sidewinders will revert to normal means of locomotion when placed on firm ground.

## Eyes

Snakes possess rather inefficient eyes considering their predatory habits. This is due to their evolutionary history, the modern snakes all having evolved from primitive burrowing forms in which the eyes were unnecessary and therefore degenerated to a point where many of the more sophisticated features found in the eyes of other reptiles were lost, never to be regained. Their main limitation is the inability to focus by changing the shape of the lens (except one species, *Dryophis nasuta*) and their perception of detail is therefore poor. They also have difficulty in noticing stationary objects but compensate for this by a keen sense of smell and, in some cases, by detecting heat generated by animals which are warmer or cooler than the surroundings (see below).

Generally speaking, burrowing and secretive species have small eyes, whereas active species have large eyes, especially those which hunt mainly by sight, e.g. many arboreal species, and fast-moving diurnal species such as the whipsnakes, genera *Coluber*, *Masticophis* and others. Another difference is found in the shape of the pupil, those of predominantly diurnal species being round whereas nocturnal species usually have vertically slit or elliptical pupils (Plates 12 and 13). However, there

Plate 12    The ribbon snake, *Thamnophis sauritus*, is an active diurnal species and has large eyes and a round pupil.

Plate 13    The reticulated python, *Python reticulatus*, is mainly nocturnal and has vertical pupils.

Plate 14   The long-nosed tree snake. *Dryophis nasuta*, is one of a small number of species with horizontal pupils. The grooves along its snout allow it to focus both eyes in a forward direction.

Plate 15   This frontal view of *Dryophis* demonstrates its binocular vision.

are exceptions: for instance, all vipers have vertical pupils, but a number of them, notably the adder, *Vipera berus*, hunt mostly during the day, probably because at the northern latitudes where it is found the nights are too cold for it, yet it retains the characteristic slit pupils as a relic of its origins amongst parent stock from warmer climes.

Tree snakes of the genera *Dryophis* and *Thelotornis* are unusual in that their pupils are horizontally slit (Plates 14 and 15). This, coupled with their pointed snout, gives them a higher degree of binocular vision, an important asset to species which hunt mainly agile lizards (and which may also need to judge the distances between the boughs and branches where they climb).

Truly fossorial (burrowing) snakes have only rudimentary eyes which may be completely covered with scales (Fig. 7).

## The Tongue and Jacobson's Organ

One of the snake's most celebrated features is its forked tongue, which it frequently protrudes through a notch in the upper jaw, the 'lingual fossa', and flickers for several seconds before it is withdrawn (Plate 16). The purpose of this action is to pick up minute particles of scent from the air and to transfer them to openings in the roof of the mouth which lead to a

Fig. 7   Head of *Typhlops* species, showing eyes covered by scales.

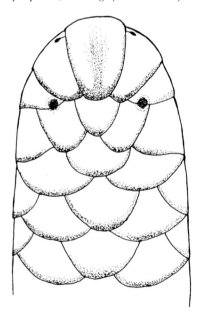

paired structure known as Jacobson's organ. This is lined with sensitive cells which in turn transmit information to the brain via a branch of the olfactory duct.

## Heat-sensitive Pits

Heat-sensitive facial pits are an extremely specialised sense organ found only in snakes belonging to two families. Of the Boidae, all pythons except the Calabar ground python, *Calabaria reinhardtii*, and a genus of Australian species, *Aspidites*, as well as three genera of boas (*Corallus* and *Epicrates* from South and Central America and *Sanzinia* from Madagascar) have these pits which are situated along the upper jaw, although their exact position varies between the sub-families: in the pythons they occur within each scale (Plate 22), whereas in the boas they are between them (Plate 23).

Vipers belonging to the sub-family Crotalinae (pit vipers), which include the American rattlesnakes, fer-de-lance and bushmaster, and the Asian bamboo and temple vipers, possess a single pair of prominent pits each located between the eye and the nostril (Plate 17). These are exceedingly sensitive to temperature changes as small as $0.2°C$, and by comparing 'messages' received on the right and left sides, the exact location of warm-blooded prey can be deduced, enabling the snakes to strike accurately even in darkness.

## Structural Adaptations to the Environment

To a large extent, the external appearance of snakes depends on the environment in which they normally live. Although many species are adaptable or 'general purpose', i.e. they can climb a little, swim a little and burrow a little, others have opted for just one niche, and in these species certain structural modifications enable them to exploit their chosen environment to the full (but also make them more or less helpless · in a strange one). Sometimes all the species in a family or sub-family pursue a single life-style, such as the exclusively burrowing thread snakes, Leptotyphlopidae, and the totally aquatic sea snakes, sub-family Hydrophinae, but other families contain a variety of types, particularly the Colubridae, which, apart from being the largest family, also occurs in the greatest diversity of habitats.

Burrowing snakes are characterised by cylindrical bodies covered in shiny scales. Their snouts may be pointed or wedge-shaped, and the rostral scale is often large (Fig. 8). Their tails are usually blunt, although the shield-tails (family Uropeltidae) have a highly specialised tail which is obliquely truncated and furnished with a number of small spines (see page 128). A few other species have tails which end in a small sharp point. Most burrowing species have small poorly-developed eyes, and in some

Plate 16  This common boa, *Boa constrictor*, is using its tongue to pick up air-borne scent particles.

Plate 17   The heat-sensitive pits of the pit vipers are situated between the eyes and nostrils: *Lachesis muta*, the bushmaster.

35

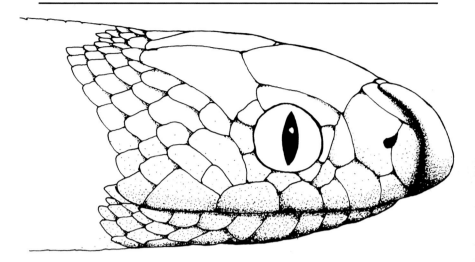

Fig. 8   The head of a typical burrowing snake, showing the enlarged rostral scale.

cases these are covered over by scales, rendering them practically non-functional. As most of them feed on soft-bodied invertebrates such as worms, termite larvae and other grubs, their mouths are small and incapable of opening widely, and some lack teeth on the upper or lower jaw. Generally speaking, burrowing snakes are small in size.

Reptiles, including snakes, have been amongst the most successful colonisers of the inhospitable desert regions of the world (due in part to the impermeable nature of their skins). Although some of the species found in these regions live beneath the surface, e.g. the sand boas, genus *Eryx*, and therefore show characteristics associated with a subterranean way of life, others live on, or just below, shifting sands and these have evolved quite differently. Most are short and stout in shape and are covered in heavily-keeled scales which give plenty of grip against an unstable substrate. They can spread their ribs to make themselves flat in cross-section with angular flanks which enable them to shuffle quickly beneath the surface, leaving only their nostrils and eyes showing. The eyes may be protected by small horn-like structures, as in the North American sidewinder, *Crotalus cerastes*, and the horned viper, *Cerastes cerastes* (Plate 18), or, alternatively, they may be situated on the top of the head as in *Bitis peringueyi*. Most are cryptically coloured to match the substrate on which they live, and as this may vary from region to region some species show a high degree of geographical variation, for instance the horned adder, *Bitis caudalis*, from South Africa, which varies in basic colour from light grey or buff to dark brown or even dark red, according to locality.

Plate 18   Horns over the eyes are found in several desert viperids, for example, the horned viper, *Cerastes cerastes*.

Aquatic snakes are usually of stout build (this gives them more thrust and less drag through the water), and their bodies are often flattened from side to side enabling them to push against a greater volume of water. For the same reason, their tails may be paddle-shaped (Fig. 9). Their eyes and nostrils are situated towards the top of their head and point upwards, and many species show counter-shading (see page 49). In a number of species the ventral scales are reduced to a narrow ridge (see under 'Locomotion'). In some highly aquatic species of snakes, the right lung extends a long way backwards and is used to adjust the buoyancy of the snake, rather as a swimbladder is used in fish.

Arboreal snakes are usually long and slender and many have prehensile tails. Because they tend to hunt fast-moving prey such as lizards and birds, they possess large efficient eyes and a number have sharply pointed snouts so that both eyes can be focused on the same object. Many are coloured green or brown to provide camouflage when they are resting amongst foliage or branches.

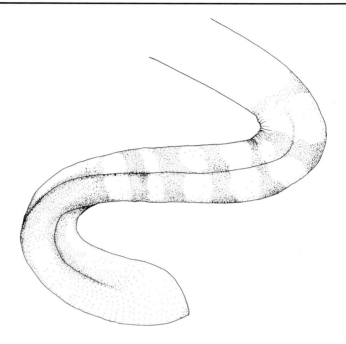

Fig. 9   The tail of most sea snakes is flattened from side to side to become paddle-shaped.

Back-fanged snakes of the genus *Chrysopelea* have gone a stage further than other arboreal snakes in having mastered, to some extent, the air. These species frequently launch themselves from a high branch and, as they do so, they change the shape of their ventral surface until it becomes slightly concave in cross-section, enabling them to glide or parachute to the ground. During their 'flight' their body undulates in much the same manner as it would if the snake were travelling across *terra firma*. One can only assume that this behaviour evolved as a means of escaping from predators.

Certain other, even more bizarre, modifications have unknown or dubious functions, and include the paired nasal 'tentacles' of the fishing snake, *Erpeton tentaculatum* (Plate 19), which were thought for a long time to act as lures for their piscine prey, a theory which has now fallen from favour, and the nasal horns found on other species, sometimes paired as in the rhinoceros viper, *Bitis nasicornis*, and, to a lesser extent, in the gaboon viper, *Bitis gabonica* (Plate 26), and sometimes single as in the vipers, *Vipera ammodytes* (Plate 20) and *V. latasti*, two Mediterranean species.

The 'rattle' found on the tip of the tail of snakes belonging to the New

Plate 19   The function of the unique 'tentacles' of the fishing snake, *Erpeton tentaculatum*, is not known.

Plate 20   The sand viper, *Vipera ammodytes*, is one of a number of *Vipera* species which have a single horn on the tip of their snouts.

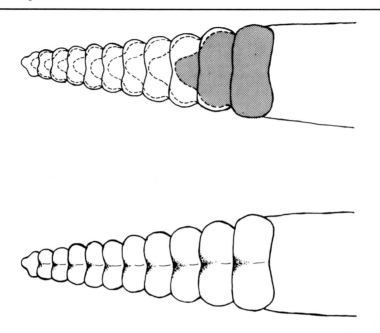

Fig. 10   The rattle on the tail of rattlesnakes consists of a series of interlocking horny rings which make a buzzing sound when the tail is vibrated rapidly.

World genera *Crotalus* (rattlesnakes) and *Sistrurus* (pigmy rattlesnakes) is a unique organ, the purpose and origin of which has been the subject of much discussion and speculation over the years. Basically, it consists of a series of horny cones, interlocking with each other by means of a constriction around their centre (Fig. 10). The young snakes are born with only a knob or 'button' at the tip of their tail (Plate 21) and by their second moult the tail tip will have shrunk away from its thick outer shell, leaving a space all around it. Because of the constriction, the old shell is held loosely in place when the rest of the skin is shed, the sloughed skin breaking off around the 'mouth' of the shell. With each successive moult a new shell is added and thus the rattle is formed. After several moults the button and the oldest segments usually break off and snakes with more than nine or ten shells are rarely found.

The purpose of the rattle, and its benefit to the snake, are not definitely established but, rather than as an audible warning, its main function is probably to focus the attention of predators and prey on to the snake's tail rather than its head. It has been suggested that the rattle may have originated as a lure, much as certain other snakes use their tails (see page 80), the banded colouration of the tails of young rattlers giving credibility

Plate 21 The rattle of a young rattlesnake. The end segment, or 'button', usually breaks off after the first six or seven moults.

to this theory. The rapid movement of the tail, instigated by any disturbance, which causes the rattling or buzzing sound, is also common to many others species of snakes, e.g. ratsnakes , genus *Elaphe*, and gopher snakes, genus *Pituophis*.

## Parallelism

Occasionally, pairs of animals which are totally unrelated taxonomically and geographically bear strong resemblances towards one another, due to similar environmental pressures being applied to both. Several good examples may be found amongst the snakes, the most remarkable probably being the almost identical appearances of the green tree python, *Chondropython viridis* (Plate 22), an Old World species from Papua New Guinea and Northern Australia, and *Corallus caninus*, the emerald tree boa (Plate 23) from South America. Although these snakes are not even in the same sub-family and live on opposite sides of the world, both are arboreal species which live in tropical rain forests. Obviously, camouflage and arboreal habits have figured importantly in the evolution of both, resulting in predominantly green snakes with prehensile tails. However,

Plate 22   The green tree python, *Chondropython viridis*, from the Australasian region. Note the position of its facial pits *within* each scale.

Plate 23    The emerald tree boa, *Corallus caninus*, is an arboreal species from South America, and is remarkably similar to *Chondropython viridis*, an example of parallel evolution, but its pits are situated *between* the labial scales.

the python has heat-sensitive pits *in* the scales bordering its upper lips, whereas in the boa these are *between* the scales.

This phenomenon is known as parallelism, or parallel evolution, and another example has already been alluded to: the sidewinding vipers, *Crotalus cerastes* and *Cerastes cerastes* from the desert regions of North America and Africa respectively. In these and in other examples, the snakes concerned not only look like one another but also behave in a similar fashion.

In summary, structural adaptations tend to be linked with a particular life-style rather than with closely related taxonomic groups of snakes. The most important modifications, with their occurrence throughout the eleven families of snakes, are shown in Table 3.

**Table 3:  Distribution of Environmental Adaptations Throughout the Families of Snakes**

| Family | Burrowing<br>Blunt snout<br>Blunt tail<br>Smooth scales<br>Cylindrical body | Aquatic<br>Stout body<br>Flattened tail<br>Nostrils pointing up<br>Eyes pointing up<br>Countershading | Arboreal<br>Slender body<br>Long prehensile tail<br>Large eyes | Mode of reproduction |
|---|---|---|---|---|
| Leptotyphlopidae | All species | | | Oviparous |
| Typhlopidae | All species | | | Oviparous |
| Anomalepidae | All species | | | Unknown |
| Uropeltidae | All species | | | Ovo-viviparous |
| Aniliidae | All species | | | Ovo-viviparous |
| Xenopeltidae | Partially | | | Unknown |
| Boidae | Some species, e.g. *Eryx, Charina, Calabaria* | Some species, e.g. *Eunectes* (partially) | Some species, e.g. *Corallus, Sanzinia, Chondropython* | Both types |
| Acrochordidae | | All species | | Ovo-viviparous |
| Colubridae | Some species, e.g. *Aparallactinae* | Some species, e.g. *Homolopsinae* | Some species, e.g. *Dipsadinae* | Mostly oviparous<br>Some ovo-viviparous<br>Few natricines viviparous |
| Elapidae | Some species, e.g. *Micrurus* | Some species, e.g. Hydrophinae, Laticaudinae and *Boulengerina* | Some species, e.g. *Dendroaspis* | N.W. species oviparous<br>Some O.W. species ovo-viviparous<br>Few Australian species viviparous |
| Viperidae | | *Agkistrodon* (partially) | Some species, e.g. *Atheris, Bothrops, Trimeresurus* | Mostly ovo-viviparous<br>Few oviparous or viviparous |

## Internal Anatomy

As is to be expected, the elongated bodies of snakes contain components which are equally elongated (Fig. 11). The lungs, for example, which in most other vertebrates are paired and of roughly equal size, take the form

Fig. 11   Internal anatomy of a snake (dorsal view) showing the position of the main organs.

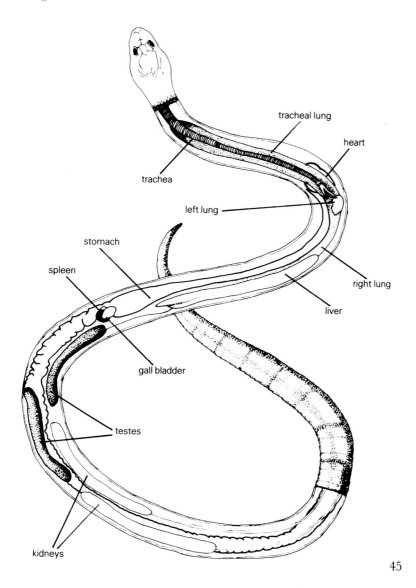

of a large right lobe, with the left lobe either absent altogether, or considerably reduced in size and practically non-functional. (The only exceptions to this layout are the single species comprising the family Xenopeltidae, *Xenopeltis unicolor*, and some members of the Boidae which have two functional lungs.) To compensate, the single lobe is rendered more efficient by extending backwards, and also forwards, where it surrounds the trachea (windpipe) and is known as the tracheal lung.

The digestive system is also modified, the stomach consisting merely of a slightly widened region of the alimentary canal, and the intestines are only slightly coiled. The elongated liver, comprising a large right and smaller left lobe, is situated alongside the lung. The gall bladder is not found within the liver but is situated behind it, opening into the small intestine just below the stomach and close to the pancreas. Similarly, the kidneys are much narrower and longer than usual (i.e. not kidney-shaped!) and are accommodated more easily by being staggered, the right being positioned further forward than the left. Except in their embryonic stages, there is no bladder as snakes do not pass liquid urine, the nitrogenous waste being excreted as uric acid crystals, a white paste which is voided with the animal's faeces.

Fig. 12   The 'claws' of pythons and boas are found on either side of the anal scale and are actually vestigial hind limbs.

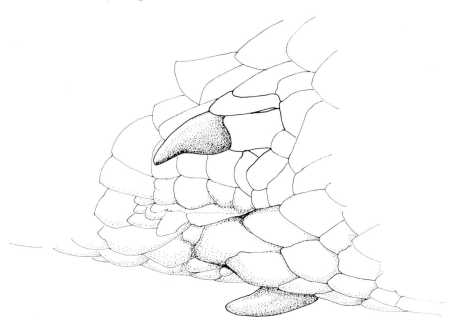

Both male and female reproductive organs are modified, the testes staggered in the same manner as the kidneys, with the right being furthest forward. The arrangement of the ovaries may be similar, or the left oviduct may be absent altogether.

The structure of the skull, although not influenced by the animal's shape, is also noteworthy on account of its great flexibility, particularly amongst members of the more advanced families, which prey upon animals that are often larger than the diameter of their own heads, but which must nevertheless be swallowed whole. Briefly, the upper and lower jaws consist of loosely connected bones which are capable of moving away from each other as well as from the cranium (the bony 'box' enclosing the brain) during the swallowing process.

Apart from the skull, the rest of the snake's skeleton consists entirely of a backbone containing from about 150 to 450 vertebrae, each associated with a pair of ribs. Each vertebra has a ball at one end and a socket at the other so that it can be articulated on its two neighbouring vertebrae, and also a number of wing-like projections, or 'processes', which interlock loosely with the corresponding processes on adjacent vertebrae in order to limit the degree to which the animal's body can be twisted or bent, thereby preventing damage to the spinal chord which runs through the backbone, or the nerves and blood vessels which are routed alongside it. A small number of snakes belonging to four of the more primitive families (Leptotyphlopidae, Typhlopidae, Aniliidae and Boidae) have, in addition to the backbone, a vestigial pelvic girdle and hind limbs (Fig. 12), relics of their evolutionary origins as lizard-like reptiles.

## Chapter 3
# Colour and Markings

Snakes are found in a variety of combinations of colours and markings – hardly any two of the 2,700 or so species are the same. These colours and patterns do not occur arbitrarily however; each has evolved to suit the particular conditions under which the various species live, and it is safe to assume that each 'design' has been perfected by the evolutionary process to be of benefit to its possessor. The purpose of this section is to examine, as far as we are able, some of the possible functions of colour and markings as used by snakes, and to see how the various types of markings fit into this picture. However, few firm lines can be drawn: certain markings may serve more than one purpose, or their function may vary from one species to another. Again, some species change their colours and/or markings as they grow, presumably as their habits and therefore their needs for camouflage etc change, whereas other species exist in more than one colour or pattern 'phase'.

## What is Colour?

Before we ask why certain colours occur, however, it would be a good idea to first consider how they are formed, but it should be made clear that only a brief and rather simplified account of this complex aspect of natural history can be given.

Colour in snakes (and other animals for that matter) may be due either to the physical nature of the surface (structural colour) or to its chemical composition (pigmentary colour). Structural colours in snakes are of two basic types: interference colour, and scattering of light (sometimes known as Tyndall colouring after its discoverer).

Interference colour is caused by the differing distances of travel involved when light is reflected from the upper and lower surfaces of a thin transparent material, such as the outer layer (epidermis) of snake skin, and is responsible for the iridescent colouration of certain snakes, as seen to good effect in d'Albertis' python, *Liasis albertisi* (Plate 79), the rainbow boa, *Epicrates cenchria* (Plate 73), the sunbeam snake, *Xenopeltis unicolor* (Plate 72), and on the shiny underside of many species. (In a more familiar context, a drop of oil on a puddle of water demonstrates this phenomenon.) The main characteristic of iridescence is that the colours change according to the angle at which light strikes the surface, relative to the observer's position. In snakes, each scale presents a separate curved facet, and so a number of colours are seen at the same time on various parts of the animal, and these change position as the animal moves, or the direction of the light or the viewpoint is altered.

Colour formed by the scattering of light, on the other hand, is not iridescent, and is caused by the scattering of short light waves (those at the blue end of the spectrum) by very small particles, as seen in the sky and in the blue eyes of humans. Amongst snakes, however, blue is a very rare colour and the explanation for this is that between the layer of small light-scattering particles and the outer surface of the skin is a layer of cells containing yellow pigment in the form of oil droplets. These cells, known as xanthophores, form a yellow filter to the blue light produced beneath them, giving the familiar green colour of various arboreal snakes, e.g. the long-nosed tree snake, *Dryophis nasuta* (Plate 25), the green tree python, *Chondropython viridis* (Plate 22), and others. Occasionally, 'blue' snakes are found in which the yellow layer is absent through mutation (see 'Aberrant colouration' below). Conversely all pigment *except* that in the xanthophores may be absent, producing a totally yellow (leucistic) individual (Plate 38).

Pigmentary colours, i.e. non-structural, are formed by the presence of various coloured chemicals within the inner layers of the animal's skin. There are a number of these and their distribution over the animal's surface obviously varies from species to species and gives to each its characteristic colours and markings. The most important of them is melanin, which comes in two main forms: eumelanin, which is black or dark brown; and phaeomelanin, which is light brown or yellowish. Grey is formed by a sparse distribution of melanin, and many more colours are formed by a combination of melanin with additional colours (structural or pigmentary). Other colours, such as red, orange, white and some yellows, can be due to a variety of pigments, such as carotenoids and guanine, but many of these have not been fully investigated or identified with reference to reptiles.

## Camouflage (Crypsis)

The vast majority of snakes have colours which help them to blend into their environment (colour resemblance), thus most terrestrial species are some shade of brown or grey (Plate 24), arboreal species may be green (but also brown if they happen to live amongst branches rather than foliage) (Plate 25), and desert species vary from yellow through to red depending on soil type. Camouflaged snakes may be plain coloured, but many are blotched or mottled, depending on their habits and habitats, and some species are marked in such a way that they exactly simulate bark, twigs etc. Highly aquatic species are, like most fish, dark above and paler below to compensate for the effect of a shadow on their underside

Plate 24    Most terrestrial snakes are predominantly brown in colour: *Nerodia cyclopion*.

Plate 25    Many arboreal snakes are also cryptically coloured: *Dryophis nasuta*.

Plate 26    The gaboon viper *Bitis gabonica*, is superbly camouflaged when resting amongst dead leaves, despite its seemingly flamboyant markings.

Plate 27    The eye of several snakes is disguised by a dark line running through it: the leopard snake, *Elaphe situla*.

Plate 28  The copperhead, *Agkistrodon contortrix*, another example of a snake which has disruptive markings. One of this group is about to shed its skin.

and thereby become less conspicious to predators level with, and beneath, them in the water, as well as from above (countershading).

## Disruptive Colouration

Many species which have camouflage colouration gain some additional measure of 'invisibility' by the arrangement of their markings in such a way as to disguise their outline (e.g. Plate 28). These markings commonly take the form of blotches, saddles or reticulations or they may be more elaborate – chevrons or zig-zig markings along their length, for instance. Occasionally, species appear to have a random collection of colours in a roughly geometrical arrangement, several of which do not match the substrate on which the snake habitually rests. These are examples of 'pure' disruptive colouration. The gaboon viper (*Bitis gabonica*) provides an excellent example of this type of concealment (Plate 26).

Disruptive markings may be concentrated around some part of the body which would normally be difficult to disguise by crypsis; for instance, many species have dark lines passing through, or radiating from, the eye, an organ which would otherwise be instantly recognisable to a predator (or prey) and could therefore give away the snake's presence and position (Plate 27).

## Warning Colour and Mimicry

A small number of snake species may be brightly coloured to 'warn' predators that they are dangerous. The American coral snakes, *Micrurus* and *Micruroides*, are obvious examples of this system. Other, harmless species from the same region, notably *Lampropeltis triangulum*, *L. zonata* and *L. pyromelana*, are coloured in exactly the same way, apparently gaining some degree of immunity by 'cashing-in' on the predators' learned response to the dangerous species (Plates 29 and 30). However, there is an obvious flaw in this argument: the coral snakes are so poisonous that they are likely to kill their attacker, therefore its 'learned' avoidance will be of no future value to the coral snakes or their mimics.

One possible solution to this problem was suggested by the German herpetologist, Robert Mertens. He found that, in parts of South and Central America, a number of mildly poisonous back-fanged snakes, for instance *Erythrolamprus aesculapii*, are also marked with the 'coral' pattern (and are therefore known as 'false' coral snakes). He concluded that animals attacking any of these species may suffer a mild bite – not enough to kill them, but sufficient to dissuade them from a repeat performance. The venomous *Micrurus* and *Micruroides*, as well as the completely harmless *Lampropeltis* and other mimics, would then both benefit from the system. This explanation has been widely accepted and is known as Mertensian mimicry, after its proposer. Once again, however, a problem exists: the mildly venomous species are restricted to South and Central America; the coral snakes and *Lampropeltis* range well into N. America – without a model the mimic cannot gain any protection, and I believe that there is another, equally plausible, explanation.

*Micrurus* species, as well as the *Lampropeltis* and other harmless species concerned, are all secretive nocturnal snakes which spend most of the daylight hours beneath the ground or under rocks and logs. Obviously, brilliant warning colouration is of little value during the night when these species are active, but it may be useful if the snakes are disturbed during the day by predators moving the object under which they are hiding or digging them up. It is easy to imagine the effect of such a brilliantly coloured snake suddenly exposed in this way – the predator will be momentarily startled, giving the snake precious moments in which it may be able to escape – an example, not of warning colouration, but of startle (or deimatic) colouration (see below).

Plate 29  A coral snake, *Micrurus lemniscatus*, a member of the cobra family and highly venomous.

Plate 30  A Kingsnake, *Lampropeltis pyromelana woodini*. Does it mimic the coral snake, or is their similarity coincidental?

## Startle Colouration

One possible instance of startle colouration is given above. Other, more widely accepted, examples are to be found amongst the snakes. North American ringneck snakes, *Diadophis*, have bright orange or red scales beneath their tails, which they raise if provoked, and a similar arrangement is found in the Asian species *Cylindrophis rufus*, the Malaysian pipe snake. Other species have brightly coloured interiors to their mouths – these are opened widely if the snake is molested. In all cases mentioned, the bright colours normally remain hidden when the snake is at rest and use of the 'startle' area is a means of defence dependent on a particular behaviour pattern (see also page 92).

## Colour Polymorphism

Polymorphism is the occurrence together *in the same locality* of two or more dissimilar forms within a species. It should not be confused with regional variations in colour or markings which, if they are significant and constant, may warrant subspecies status, nor with slight differences in colour or markings which are invariably present in any population of animals, nor differences in colour between the male and female of a species (which is known as sexual dimorphism). Finally, colour polymorphism does not apply to occasional mutations, such as albinism or melanism, unless these can be shown to exist at a more or less constant level within a population under natural conditions.

Several examples of colour polymorphism amongst snakes may be given, but the best known is undoubtedly that of the Californian kingsnake, *Lampropeltis getulus californiae*. This subspecies, which occurs over much of Utah, Nevada and Arizona, as well as most of California, is typically a black or dark brown snake with a series of broad white to cream bands circling its body from head to tail (Plate 31). In one small part of its range, however (in the vicinity of San Diego), a second form exists side by side with this banded 'phase'. These specimens are also marked in similar colours but the white markings, instead of being arranged across the body, take the form of a single line running the length of the snake, along its dorsal midline (Plate 32). These forms were originally thought to represent totally different species, *L. boylii* (banded) and *L. californiae* (striped), until it was shown that both types can hatch from a single clutch of eggs and both forms can breed together. (Nevertheless, banded individuals from other parts of the range, if mated with the striped form, give rise to intermediate offspring – broken bands and stripes, not the two parent types. However, as this is an artificial occurrence, the genetic reasons for this do not concern us here.) The biological significance for this phenomenon is not easy to establish but may go something like this: predators in the region may build up a mental picture of what their prey should look like (this has been proven for many

55

Plates 31 and 32   The two phases of the Californian kingsnake, *Lampropeltis getulus californiae*, may be produced from a single clutch of eggs.

types of predators). Animals which do not match this 'prey-image' are not immediately recognised as food and therefore gain some measure of immunity. In the kingsnake's case, predator A may have a prey-image of a banded snake, in which case the striped individuals are overlooked. Predator B, on the other hand, may have a prey-image of a striped snake, and the banded individuals escape notice. In general, predators build up a prey-image of the most abundant phase and the less common one benefits until *it* becomes the most common. The predator then switches its attention accordingly, and, in the long term, polymorphism is maintained within the population.

## Pattern Changes with Age

A number of species of snakes undergo pattern or colour changes as they grow. A common transition is from a blotched to a plain or striped pattern, as may be seen in several members of the genus *Elaphe* (rat snakes). Young animals in this genus are often marked with bold saddles of black or grey which gradually disappear with age to give way to a series of longitudinal lines (e.g. *E. quatuorlineata*, Plates 33 and 34, and *E. obsoleta quadrivittata*). Alternatively, the areas between the blotches become progressively darker with each slough, eventually uniting to give a uniform colouration (e.g. *E. obsoleta obsoleta*). It seems logical to suppose that the juvenile and adult types of markings give a measure of camouflage or disruptive colouration coinciding with different stages in the animal's life. It is interesting to note that this phenomenon is shown by species of *Elaphe* occurring in both the New World and the Old.

A more dramatic change of appearance occurs in the Australasian snake *Chondropython viridis*, in which juveniles are brilliant yellow in colour (Plate 35) and the adults are green. In this instance it is difficult to see the benefit of the juvenile colouration, although the green of the adult clearly provides good camouflage for this arboreal species.

## Colour Aberrants

In snakes, as in most other groups of animals, occasional mutations give rise to abnormally-coloured individuals. The most obvious examples of this are the appearance from time to time of albino animals (lacking pigment and therefore appearing white or pink) (Plates 36 and 38) and melanistic animals (totally black owing to an abundance of the black pigment, melanin, which obscures all the other colours and markings). Other types of colour mutation include leucistic (yellow) and erythrocystic (red) individuals and all four of these mutations have occasionally been reported in wild snakes (Plate 37). For some strange reason, these abnormal animals have become highly prized and are often selectively bred in zoos and large private collections. A further type of variation

Plate 33    Juvenile four-lined snakes, *Elaphe quatuorlineata* are heavily blotched.

Plate 34    The same snake, now half-grown, has begun to develop stripes, whilst the blotches are fading.

Plate 36 (right)    An albino cobra, *Naja naja* – it has no pigment at all, the eyes being coloured pink by numerous small blood vessels.

Plate 37 (far right)    A leucistic Indian python – only the layer of oil droplets just beneath the surface contains pigments. Compare this and the next plate with Plate 78.

Plate 35    Juvenile *Chondropython viridis* are yellow (sometimes brick-red) at hatching and change to the green colour of the adults (Plate 22) at about two years of age.

Plate 38   This Indian python, *Python molurus*, is a partial albino – ite eyes and some of its scales contain pigment.

involves the absence of just one or more pigments and this may have a dramatic effect – the green colouration of some snakes is achieved by a combination of blue and yellow (see page 49) and if the yellow layer is lacking, as sometimes occurs in, for example, the green tree python, *Chondropython viridis*, the snake is bright blue. In nature, the greater majority of these mutants would soon fall prey, lacking as they do any of the advantages of crypsis etc. In a few cases, melanism may be slightly advantageous under certain conditions and the characteristic may spread throughout a population: the garter snakes, *Thamnophis sirtalis*, which occur around Lake Erie and in parts of Nova Scotia in Canada are a case in point – a high proportion of these individuals are black, a situation which has probably come about because, at this northerly latitude, the marginally greater heat absorption associated with black colouration counterbalances their slightly more conspicuous appearance. (Vipers, *Vipera berus*, which occur towards the north of this species' range, also tend towards melanism, 'black adders' being quite frequent in certain localities.) It should also be pointed out that isolated colonies, such as those living on islands, are more liable to contain a proportion of abnormally-coloured individuals, due partly to the lack of large predators and partly to the small 'gene pool' and the subsequent high incidence of inbreeding.

*Chapter 4*

# Reproduction

The most powerful motivation common to all organisms is to reproduce, for only by doing so can their genes survive. Snakes are no exception to this rule and although they may appear to spend much of their time pursuing other activities, such as basking, hunting or feeding, all of these functions are directed towards attaining a level of fitness which will enable them to find a mate and produce the living material for the next generation.

## Breeding Cycles

Breeding cycles vary according to whether the species in question hails from a temperate (cool) climate or a tropical one. Temperate species of snakes normally fall into an annual or biennial reproductive pattern, mating in spring or early summer, producing their eggs or young by the end of the summer and replacing food reserves before hibernation in the autumn. During hibernation, the sex cells (spermatozoa and ova) develop and the cycle repeats itself the following year, although species with a short season of activity may require a 'fallow' year (or possibly two) in which to recover their fitness. There may be variations within this schedule – females occasionally mate before hibernation and some species, which hibernate in large aggregations, may mate *en masse* as soon as they emerge and before their dispersal throughout the surrounding country-side; for instance, garter snakes (*Thamnophis sirtalis*) from northern parts of the species' range, e.g. in Canada, often form enormous mating aggregations consisting of several hundred males, all attempting to mate with a small number of females (Plate 39).

Onset of the mating drive in temperate regions may be initiated in the spring by rising temperatures or increasing day length or both. The temperature is likely to fluctuate from day to day due to vagaries in the weather and is therefore not the most reliable indicator of the season, whereas day length tends to be more constant for a given part of the year. It has been shown experimentally for some species of reptiles (mostly lizards) that day length is the most important environmental cue but that temperature also has some bearing on it; in other words, a certain minimum temperature has to prevail before breeding can begin, irrespective of day length. It should be borne in mind that a number of snakes,

61

Plate 39  *Thamnophis sirtalis parietalis*, a subspecies of the common garter snake, sometimes forms breeding aggregations numbering several hundreds (simulated photograph).

including some temperate ones, are largely fossorial or nocturnal, and it would seem unlikely that they are influenced to any great extent by day length, but thorough investigations into the breeding cycles of these animals have not yet been carried out.

A number of instances are on record of females producing eggs or young without having mated that season. These are due to the storing of sperm from a previous mating (*amphigonia retardata*), but fertility is often diminished and females will mate every year given the chance. Certain species are capable of producing two or more clutches in a single year, at least under ideal captive conditions, and it seems likely that this happens occasionally in the wild during 'good' years, but it can be somewhat difficult to establish whether this is so, or how frequently it occurs. In particular, it would be difficult to ascertain whether both clutches are the result of a single mating, or if the female mates again after laying the first clutch.

In the tropics, breeding may still be seasonal, but cues are often more subtle, and may be connected to rainfall, humidity and the abundance of certain prey species. Other tropical species may breed throughout the year but peaks of breeding may be reached during certain months. Again, even in those species where gravid females may be found at any time of the year, it does not follow that each one breeds more than once each year – within a population the breeding cycles of individuals may be staggered.

## Courtship and Mating

Courtship in snakes is unspectacular compared with other groups of vertebrates. They do not possess the frills, crests or bright colours needed for visual display (their sight is poorly developed), nor do they sing or call to their mates and rivals (they are practically deaf as well). For these reasons, their courtship has attracted little attention from biologists: this does not, however, make it any less important to them!

Males appear to be attracted to their mates by a scent trail left by a female in reproductive condition. The scent is produced primarily from the anal gland, but also from the female's skin (females often seem to be more attractive to males immediately after they have sloughed). When the male tracks down the female he will try to stimulate her by rubbing his chin, on which there are a number of small tubercles, over the lower part of her back. She may respond by twitching or jerking her body, and as he crawls forward this becomes more vigorous, assuming that she is recep- tive. Eventually, their cloacae are in close proximity, they twist their tails together and a connection is made via one of the male's paired copulatory organs, the hemipenes, which are normally inverted (turned inside-out) and rest in a cavity at the base of his tail. In pythons and boas, the claw-like vestigial limbs of the male, situated at either side of the cloaca, may be used to scratch or 'tickle' the female's sides.

The pair may remain joined for a few minutes or several hours, and, should the female move about, the male, which is usually smaller, may be dragged along too. After mating has been completed, the pair normally disperse, although there is evidence that in a few species they remain together for a time afterwards, possibly until egg-laying takes place.

After mating, males of some species form 'copulation plugs'. These consist of a mass of waxy material which remains in the cloaca of the female for 2–4 days after mating and then falls out. Its function may be to prevent leakage of the sperm from the female's reproductive tract, or it may prevent a rival male from mating with her immediately afterwards and so diluting the sperm from the first male. The latter explanation seems most likely, since males do not guard their mates as most vertebrates do to prevent promiscuity. So far, these plugs have only been found in a few species of closely related species of the sub-family Natricinae, all of which occur in quite dense aggregations for a few days immediately after hibernation when mating activity is at a peak.

It remains to be seen which other snakes form plugs and, if so, whether *their* behaviour during the breeding season would also favour this 'enforced chastity' mechanism.

## Parthenogenesis

Parthenogenesis is the term given to a method of reproduction in which the egg-cell (ovum) begins to divide and develop without the necessity of fertilisation by a male sperm cell. Females of parthenogenetic species are therefore able to produce offspring without having mated but, since there is no male parent, the young will have no male chromosomes and will all be females (who will in time also be capable of reproducing parthenogenetically and so on).

Parthenogenesis is quite common amongst invertebrates and it also occurs in a few species of fish and lizards but, as far as is known, only one species of snake, the Brahminy blind snake, *Rhamphotyphlops braminus* (Plate 71), reproduces in this way. This diminutive burrowing species is known from a large number of specimens, all of which are female, a good indication that it is parthenogenetic, although until females which are reared in isolation are shown to be capable of laying fertile eggs it is difficult to be 100 per cent certain.

Because parthenogenetic species are able to establish new colonies following the introduction of just one individual (conventional species require at least one male and one female, or a pregnant female), they tend to be more successful in extending their ranges, and this is certainly true of *R. braminus*: it has been collected from such far-flung places as Africa, India, Sri Lanka, many Pacific islands, South-east Asia, Australia, Hawaii and Mexico, and since it seems likely that it reached many of these by unintentionally stowing away amongst the roots of plants as they were transported around the world it is often known appropriately as the 'flowerpot snake'.

## Egg-laying and Birth

The gestation period of snakes varies from species to species, and also according to the prevailing conditions, especially temperature, and can be difficult to calculate anyway as fertilisation does not always occur at the time of mating. Table 4 (p. 69) gives the gestation periods, along with other reproductive data, for a selection of common snakes, obtained from captive specimens, where conditions are more or less constant.

In a number of species, the eggs are retained within the body of the female until development is well advanced. This may result in a long gestation followed by a short incubation period, or, in extreme cases, the hatching of the eggs before they are laid, or immediately afterwards. In most cases, the eggs are covered in a thin membrane which allows the transfer of water and oxygen to the developing embryos, but since no other nutrients are obtained in this way from the mother, this method of reproduction should, strictly speaking, be termed ovo-viviparity. There is evidence of true viviparity, characterised by the presence of a placenta, in very few snakes. Examples are the European adder, *Vipera berus*, and at least one member of the Australian genus *Denisonia*.

There is no evidence of parental care amongst ovo-viviparous snakes; the young, having freed themselves from the membrane, disperse and begin a completely independent existence.

Oviparous snakes lay elongated eggs, covered with a thick, but pliable, shell through which water and oxygen can pass to the developing embryo. The shells are usually white or cream in colour and their surface may be slightly granular or covered with fine ridges and reticulations, species which are closely related often having similar eggs. In nature, the eggs are laid in a place where they can absorb sufficient moisture for their development, but where the risk of predation is minimal. Cavities in rotting logs, and piles of decaying vegetation are often chosen and such materials may also help to speed up the development by means of the heat generated through their decomposition. The females appear to have a good 'nose' for suitable places as only rarely are clutches discovered, even in places where snakes are known to be abundant. Occasionally, a shortage of good sites causes a number of females to deposit their clutches near one another, and since most of these are likely to hatch at around the same time a glut, or 'plague', of baby snakes may occur, often to the delight of the local press.

Snake eggs are slightly sticky when first laid and may adhere to each other, so that the clutch forms an irregular mass. The majority of species take no further interest in their eggs once they are laid, but a few instances of clutch-guarding are well documented. The small thread snake, *Leptotyphlops dulcis*, coils around its eggs in underground chambers, whereas king cobras, *Ophiophagus hannah*, are reported to drive intruders away from the area where their eggs are laid. The most highly developed guarding behaviour is found amongst pythons, especially the Indian python, *P. molurus*, which remains coiled around her eggs throughout the incubation, leaving them only occasionally to eat or drink. This may serve to camouflage the eggs, which would otherwise form a large, white, conspicuous mass, but there is also good reason to believe that the temperature of the eggs can be elevated by a physiological process not yet fully understood, but associated with regular twitching movements characteristic of brooding females. Other species of *Python* also coil around their eggs, but appear not to share the ability of raising their temperature.

During incubation all snake eggs swell, sometimes even doubling their original volume, but just before hatching they often shrivel slightly around the young snake as it uses up the yolk. The hatching process is often prolonged, the snake slashing at the shell with its egg-tooth in

Plate 40  Black ratsnake, *Elaphe obsoleta*, in the process of hatching.

several places to create an exit (Plate 40), but it often remains within the security of the shell for several hours or even days before venturing out completely. By this stage the yolk has been drawn into the snake's body, leaving a small scar on its ventral surface. The young snake rarely takes food for the first few days, and invariably sloughs its skin for the first time within a week to ten days of hatching.

## Eggs or Young?

Some species of snakes give birth to living young, whereas others lay eggs. Obviously each method of reproduction is successful for those species which practise it, so how have the two strategies evolved?

Oviparity has the advantage that the gestation period is quite short, and so the female is hindered by her burden of eggs for the minimum amount of time. She may also be able to produce more eggs than she would living young because the eggs take up less space than young, and she may be able to produce more than one clutch of eggs per season.

However, ovo-viviparity also has advantages. The developing young

66

are not as prone to predation or attack by mould as eggs are, and the female can move herself, and therefore her developing brood, from cool to warm places and thereby provide the best available environment for them at all times.

Depending on the circumstances, some species would gain an overall advantage by being ovo-viviparous, others would not. Ovo-viviparity is a fairly advanced development in the evolution of snakes (all of the primitive species lay eggs), and so it is interesting to speculate on the possible reasons for it.

a)  The ability to keep the embryos as warm as possible is of special importance to those species living in cool places – ovo-viviparity is more frequent amongst those species living away from the tropics and at high altitudes.

b)  Highly aquatic species are often ovo-viviparous, because this obviates the necessity of crawling onto the land (where many of them are almost helpless) in order to lay eggs.

c)  Highly arboreal species are often ovo-viviparous, eliminating the need for them to come down to ground level to lay eggs.

d)  Aggressive or venomous species are expert at protecting themselves, and therefore their developing young, from predators, whereas their eggs would be more difficult to protect.

e)  Heavy-bodied species, which are normally sluggish and rely on camouflage rather than speed, are inconvenienced less by the growing embryos than those which are slender and fast-moving.

Superimposed on these factors is the tendency for ovo-viviparity to have evolved in certain families and sub-families.

| | | |
|---|---|---|
| 1) | Leptotyphlopidae: | all oviparous. |
| 2) | Typhlopidae: | predominantly oviparous but two (*Typhlops diardi* and *T. bibronii*) appear to be at least partially ovo-viviparous. |
| 3) | Anomalepidae: | reproduction apparently unknown. |
| 4) | Uropeltidae: | all ovo-viviparous as far as is known. |
| 5) | Aniilidae: | all ovo-viviparous as far as is known. |
| 6) | Xenopeltidae: | reproduction apparently unknown. |
| 7) | Boidae: | boas ovo-viviparous; pythons oviparous. |
| 8) | Acrochordidae: | all species ovo-viviparous (totally aquatic). |
| 9) | Colubridae: | predominantly oviparous but with some exceptions: genera *Psammodynastes*, *Tachymenis*, *Coronella austriaca*, *Duberria*, *Pseudaspis*, *Conopsis*, *Toluca*, *Meizodon*, *Helicops*, *Elaphe rufidorsata*, nine genera of North American semi-aquatic species, all species of the aquatic sub-family Homalopsinae. |

67

10)   Elapidae:            most Australian species are ovo-viviparous, as
                           are all species of the aquatic sub-family Hyd-
                           rophinae (sea-snakes) and one genus in Africa
                           (*Haemachatus*); otherwise oviparous.

11)   Viperidae:           predominantly ovo-viviparous with some ex-
                           ceptions: two species of *Vipera*, some *Echis*
                           species, all *Causus* species, *Lachesis muta*, some
                           *Agkistrodon* and some Old World members of
                           the genus *Trimeresurus*.

## Productivity

Most species of snakes produce between three and sixteen eggs or young
per brood. A few species regularly exceed this, and a very small number
are capable, on rare occasions, of producing 100 or more offspring. These
extremely prolific species include the puff adder, *Bitis arietans*; fer-de-
lance, *Bothrops atrox*; mole snake, *Pseudaspis cana*; eastern garter snake,
*Thamnophis sirtalis*; green water snake, *Nerodia cyclopion*; and the three
largest pythons, the reticulated, *P. reticulatus*; the Indian, *P. molurus*; and
the African, *P. sebae*. Of these, the last three lay eggs, and the rest give
birth to living young. It should be emphasised that a more usual
complement of eggs for any of these species would be nearer to 50 than
100.

At the other end of the scale, a number of small species, such as the
black-headed snakes, genus *Tantilla*, and many tropical species, only
produce one to three eggs at a time, but because they live in places where
climatic conditions allow for year-round activity it seems likely that they
lay more than one clutch each year, with an almost continuous breeding
cycle in some cases, and so their total productivity throughout the year
may approach, or equal, that of species having larger clutches.

The other main factors which affect brood-size (i.e. other than number
of clutches per year) are size of species, age and size of individual, and
food availability for the young. Broadly speaking, larger species produce
more offspring than smaller ones, and, within each species, larger females
produce more young than smaller ones (young females breeding for the
first time may have broods well below average for their species and each
offspring may also be small). The other consideration is the availability of
suitably-sized prey for the young: in order to produce large broods, the
size of individuals must suffer, as a female can only hold a certain total
mass of eggs or young (approximately 20 per cent of her body weight).
Now, if the young are to feed on a type of prey which exists in small
'packages', e.g. earthworms, tadpoles or young fish, they can 'afford' to be
smaller in size, and therefore greater in number, than young which feed on
rodents, for instance, where even the smallest prey item is quite a
mouthful.

## Table 4: Reproductive Data for a Selection of Snakes

| Species | No. eggs/young | Gestation* | Incubation** |
|---|---|---|---|
| **Boidae** | | | |
| *Boa constrictor* | 20–50 | 100–150 days | ovo-viviparous |
| *Corallus enhydris* | 7–20 | c. 200 days | ovo-viviparous |
| *Lichanura trivirgata* | 4–10 | 120–135 days | ovo-viviparous |
| *Python molurus* | 20–60 | 90–130 days | 50–60 days |
| *Python sebae* | 20–60 | ? | 80–90 days |
| *Liasis childreni* | 8–10 | c. 80 days | 50–67 days |
| **Colubridae** | | | |
| *Boaedon fuliginosus* | 9–12 | 70–85 days | 60–70 days |
| *Elaphe guttata* | 8–16 | 30–50 days | 61–62 days |
| *Elaphe obsoleta* | 8–15 | 39–50 days | 68–77 days |
| *Elaphe quatuorlineata* | 5–8 | c. 70 days | 55–65 days |
| *Lampropeltis getulus* | 6–12 | c. 42 days | 50–74 days |
| *Natrix natrix* | 30–40 | 60–70 days | 40–55 days |
| *Nerodia sipedon* | 20–40 | c. 100 days | ovo-viviparous |
| *Pituophis melanoleucus* | 6–12 | c. 40 days | 63–69 days |
| *Thamnophis sirtalis* | 10–25 | 90–100 days | ovo-viviparous |
| **Elapidae** | | | |
| *Naja haje* | 15–20 | 53–80 days | 62–77 days |
| *Micrurus fulvius* | 7–9 | ? | c. 47 days |
| **Viperidae** | | | |
| *Agkistrodon rhodostoma* | 13–30 | ? | 37–47 days |
| *Crotalus atrox* | 8–12 | ? | ovo-viviparous |
| *Crotalus viridis* | 7–12 | 150–170 days | ovo-viviparous |
| *Lachesis muta* | 10–12 | ? | 73–76 days |
| *Trimeresurus albolabris* | 15–20 | 278–292 days | ovo-viviparous |
| *Trimeresurus flavoviridis* | 6–12 | 70–80 days | 40–41 days |
| *Vipera berus* | 5–15 | 100–150 days | viviparous |

* Gestation periods are difficult to calculate accurately because females may mate several times over a period of days or weeks. Furthermore, the sperm may be stored for some time before ovulation occurs.

** Incubation period depends on temperature and is therefore also prone to some variation.

Plate 41 (overleaf)   A young corn snake, *Elaphe guttata*. Because of its small size, its diet will differ slightly from that of the adult.

Compare, for example, the European grass snake, *Natrix natrix*, which averages 30–40 eggs, with the similarly-sized *Elaphe quatuorlineata* from the same region, which lays only about six eggs. The young of the former, although quite small at hatching, are capable of tackling their preferred prey, tadpoles, whereas the young four-lined snakes must, of necessity, be quite large and powerful in order to subdue and swallow the small rodents and birds which form *their* main prey.

## Growth and Development

For the most part, young snakes, whether born or hatched, are small replicas of their parents, and behave in much the same way, but a number of species have distinct juvenile forms in which the colour and markings are totally different from those of the adults (see pages 57 and Plates 33–35). With a number of species, the usual food of the adults is too large to be captured and swallowed by the young and they may have dissimilar prey preferences, with a change-over at some time during their growth (thus eliminating the problem of size discussed above). For instance, young corn snakes, *Elaphe guttata*, may feed largely on small frogs and lizards initially, before graduating to rodents, and several other species may start off by eating invertebrates, which are usually plentiful and relatively defenceless (Plate 41).

Growth rate is dependent upon two things: temperature and availability of food. The temperature will control the amount of time during which the snake can be active, and therefore, indirectly, its food intake, and so snakes from warm climates normally grow faster, and mature earlier, than those from cooler areas, all other things being equal. Food availability is dependent upon the time of hatching or birth, and most reproductive cycles are geared to this; for instance, young garter snakes, *Thamnophis*, are born at a time of the year when frogs and toads are metamorphosing in large quantities, but this aspect may also be at the mercy of other environmental factors, some years being noticeably better than others as far as the young snakes' survival is concerned. In temperate regions it is particularly important that the young snakes find sufficient food before entering their first period of hibernation, and if a cool summer results in delayed birth or hatching, this may not be possible and high mortality will result. (Grass snakes, *Natrix natrix*, however, appear not to feed on hatching but hibernate almost immediately and commence feeding the following spring.)

Superimposed on these two factors there may be an element of genetic control. It is often noticeable that a brood of young snakes reared under identical conditions will grow at different rates. All will be healthy and feed well, but one or more may grow much more slowly than the others, and 'super-growers' may also be present.

Unlike most animals, which reach a maximum size shortly after they become sexually mature, snakes continue to grow throughout their lives, although their growth rate slows down dramatically after the first few years. Most species begin to reproduce when they achieve approximately half of their eventual maximum size, the first clutch or brood being quite small, increasing gradually until, by their third or fourth reproductive season, they approach their full reproductive potential.

## Sloughing

As a snake grows it periodically sloughs or moults the outer layer of its skin – 'ecdysis' is the scientific term for this process. Unlike insects, which go through a predetermined number of moults until they reach the adult, or imago, stage, sloughing in snakes continues throughout the animal's life. It occurs about once every two months on average, but the exact frequency depends to some extent on the age, growth rate and metabolism of the individual concerned – young animals grow more rapidly and therefore slough more frequently than older ones, and sloughing ceases altogether during a period of inactivity such as hibernation.

Ecdysis is preceded by the secretion of fluid between the old layer of

Plate 42    A few days prior to sloughing, a milky fluid is secreted between the old and new layers of epidermis, making the eyes opaque and the markings dull: Californian kingsnake, striped phase.

Plate 43   Sloughing gets under way when the old epidermis is freed from the snout and chin. Note the 'spectacles' coming away with the old skin in this sand viper, *Vipera ammodytes*.

Plate 44   The snake, in this case a four-lined snake, crawls out of its old skin, turning it inside out in the process. Note that the freshly uncovered markings are brighter.

epidermis and the new one beneath it. This causes the animal's colour and pattern to become dull, and its eyes appear to swell and take on a milky appearance (Plate 42). The snake may become secretive, nervous and irritable, presumably because it is unable to see properly and feels vulnerable, and it usually abstains from food during this time. Two or three days later the eyes clear, and then, after a further four or five days, the skin is sloughed, usually in one piece.

The actual sloughing begins around the animal's snout after this has been rubbed repeatedly against a rough surface, such as a rock. The skin is then worked back over the head (Plate 43) and by crawling across an uneven substrate, or through dense grass etc, the whole skin is rolled back along the body until the snake is completely clear of it (Plate 44). It will be slightly longer than the snake, due to stretching, and inside out, but every scale of the snake's body will be visible, including those covering the eyes. Although most of the snake's pigment is contained in the layer beneath the epidermis, a faint trace of the pattern may be visible in the old skin.

After sloughing, the snake's markings will be bright and clear, and its surface will be glossy or satiny, depending on species. If it has not fed during the pre-slough period, it will be hungry and alert for signs of a potential meal, and if it is a female it will be particularly attractive to any male snake in the neighbourhood, probably due to secretions of hormone which coincide with sloughing.

Apart from the usual reason for sloughing, i.e. to accommodate growth, snakes may slough at other times: newly hatched individuals invariably slough within a week or so; animals which hibernate slough as soon as they emerge in the spring; and females slough just prior to laying their eggs. Sick or injured snakes may slough more frequently than usual, perhaps because their physiological timetables are upset, and sloughing also gives temporary respite from the attentions of ectoparasites, such as ticks and mites, which sometimes affect snakes.

## Chapter 5
# Foods and Feeding

The means by which snakes find, overpower and consume their prey are amongst the most fascinating aspects of their biology. In order to compensate for their lack of limbs, and their poor sight and hearing, a number of specialised organs and techniques have been developed which have few parallels throughout the rest of the animal kingdom, and although their ability to catch and kill prey is frequently sensationalised, there is no doubt that many have reached the peak of efficiency in this department.

## Types of Prey

All snakes are carnivorous. On the odd occasion when vegetable material has been found in their stomachs, the most likely explanation is that it was accidentally ingested along with a previous owner, as part of *its* stomach contents – an instant food-chain! Snakes are unable to dismember their prey and must swallow it whole, so in general small species eat small prey and large species eat large prey, and collectively the animals preyed upon range from ants to antelopes, depending mainly upon the size of the snake, especially its mouth, and also upon prey availability (which is in turn controlled by its habitat and range).

Although some snakes will attack just about anything of a suitable size, many species specialise to a certain extent in a single group of prey-species, for instance frogs, lizards, mammals etc, and only rarely do they take other types of animals. A few are highly specialised and are strictly limited to one or two species and may show morphological and/or behavioural adaptations which enable them to exploit these to the full.

Invertebrates are eaten by a large number of snakes. Small species, especially burrowers such as *Leptotyphlops* species are limited to prey such as termites and are frequently found living in termite nests, apparently immune to attack by the insects due to pheromone secretions which confuse them. Because their jaws are rigid, the soft parts of the prey are sucked or squeezeed out and the exoskeleton is discarded. Small colubrid snakes such as *Storeria* and *Diadophis* species are also fond of inverte-brates, especially worms and slugs, and these may also form the prey of the young of larger species such as the garter snakes, genus *Thamnophis*, which graduate to larger prey later in life. Two sub-families of colubrids, the

Dipsinae from Central and South America, and the Pareinae from Asia, specialise in eating land molluscs, including snails, which they extract from their shells by thrusting their elongated lower jaw forward and hooking their teeth into the soft part of the animal which is gradually pulled out as it is swallowed (Plate 45). An African species, *Duberria lutrix*, also eats snails but it breaks their shells by smashing them on the ground after the fleshy part has been seized. A number of snakes feed on orthopterans such as crickets and grasshoppers and these include the North American green snakes, *Opheodryas* (Plate 46), and the European meadow viper, *Vipera ursinii*. Semi-aquatic colubrids of the genus *Regina* feed almost exclusively on crayfish and other aquatic invertebrates.

Fish are eaten mainly by aquatic and semi-aquatic snakes such as the sea snakes, sub-family Hydrophiinae, the wart snakes, family Acrochordidae, colubrids of the sub-family Homolopsinae, and most of the Natricinae which includes the European and North American 'water' snakes, *Natrix* and *Nerodia* species and the garter snakes, *Thamnophis* species.

Members of the Natricinae also eat adult and larval newts, frogs and toads (in keeping with their semi-aquatic habits) and amphibians also form the diet of many other colubrids, notably the hog-nosed snakes, *Heterodon* species, which feed almost entirely on toads. A number of arboreal snakes, including the young of large species such as green tree pythons, *Chondropython viridis*, prey upon tree-frogs, and a few species, such as the cat-eyed snake, *Leptodeira*, may also take the eggs of frogs which breed on leaves, for instance the glass frogs, *Centrolenella*, and the leaf-folding frogs, *Phyllomedusa* and *Agalychnis*.

Lizards form the prey of many snakes, particularly the fast-moving diurnal species such as whipsnakes, *Coluber* and *Masticophis*, but also of nocturnal prowlers such as the cowl snake, *Macroprotodon cucullatus*, and the European cat snake, *Telescopus fallax*, which search beneath rocks for lizards that are comatose. In parts of Mexico, the strange two-legged worm-lizards, *Bipes canaliculatus*, are preyed on by coral snakes, especially *Micrurus laticollaris*, which apparently track them through their burrow systems by following pheromone trails.

Snakes are widely eaten, and several species specialise in them. The king cobra, *Ophiophagus hannah*, eats exclusively other species of snakes (its generic name indicates this), and many others, including the pipe snakes, *Cylindrophis*, and some coral snakes, *Micrurus*, feed predominantly on them. Some subspecies of the North American kingsnakes, *Lampropeltis*, include snakes along with lizards and mammals in their diet, frequently taking rattlesnakes in areas where these are abundant.

Anacondas, *Eunectes murinus*, probably the world's most powerful constrictor, are reputed to attack and eat caimans, which share their swampy habitat.

Birds are not easily preyed upon by snakes due to the obvious difficulties in catching them, although nocturnal species often take

Plate 45  *Sibon nebulata*, a Trinidadian snake which specialises in eating slugs and snails.

Plate 46  Many small snakes, such as these rough green snakes, *Opheodryas aestivus*, are insectivores.

roosting birds if the opportunity arises, and the young of ground-nesting species may form an important, but seasonal, part of the diet of some snakes. Arboreal snakes may rob nests of eggs or young and some species, for instance the Lataste's viper, *Vipera latastei*, take to climbing in low shrubs during the spring, presumably for this reason. Although many snakes, e.g. rat snakes, *Elaphe*, will eat eggs opportunistically, one genus of colubrids, *Dasypeltis*, has specialised in eating them and eats nothing else. These African snakes are able to spread their jaws to enormous proportions and, having engulfed the egg, employ downward-pointing extensions of their neck vertebrae to saw through the shell. The contents are then swallowed, and the collapsed shell is regurgitated.

Mammals, because of their large size-range and abundance, are widely preyed upon by snakes. Rodents form the main diet of numerous species from several families in both the New and Old Worlds. Young snakes and small species may be restricted by their size to newly born mice etc, which their slender cylindrical shape enables them to seek out in burrows and nests, but the giant snakes can deal with mammals up to the size of small wild pigs and deer. Domestic animals are not ignored, and dogs and cats, as well as young goats, are occasionally taken, but this loss is more than off-set by the reduction of pests around farms and human habitation. Unfortunately, this fact is rarely recognised, and harmless, as well as venomous, species are invariably persecuted. Few snakes grow large enough to eat humans, although there are one or two reliable accounts of children being taken by pythons.

Finally, it should be noted that many snakes will eat prey which is already dead, should the opportunity arise. This fact has been largely obscured in the past because food preferences of the various species were established by the examination of stomach contents: as will be appreciated, it is difficult under these circumstances to differentiate between freshly killed prey and carrion. It is now well-known that many captive snakes actually prefer dead prey, and reports of wild snakes eating, for instance, road-kills, appear from time to time. Since smell is the most important means of identifying prey, it is reasonable to assume that dead animals are perfectly acceptable, the main limitation on this source of food being competition from other scavengers, especially certain birds, which are better equipped to locate it.

## Hunting Strategy

Broadly speaking, snakes employ two types of hunting strategy: 'sit and wait' or 'seek and chase'. 'Seek and chase' species are in the minority – not many snakes are fast enough to run down prey animals such as lizards or rodents, but species such as the whipsnakes, *Coluber* and *Masticophis*, and the sand snakes, *Psammophis*, may move about flushing prey from the undergrowth or from amongst rocks and then pursuing it for short distances. These species rely heavily on sight for the detection and capture of prey. Of course, those species which eat such items as slugs, snails and earthworms have little need for great speed, and merely line up the prey so that it can be grasped in a position which is suitable for swallowing. The energy thus expended is minimal, but so is the nutritional value of the food and so these species must eat frequently.

Most species, however, prefer to loaf about in places where their chosen prey is likely to pass by and then to stalk and strike at it before their presence has been suspected. Their camouflaged markings and ability to remain motionless for long periods of time is of great value to these species, and lizards, frogs and rodents often approach close enough to be taken with a single lunge or strike. If this is unsuccessful, the snake may pursue the prey for a second attempt or it may re-position itself in readiness for the next intended victim. If prey does not come along after a certain period, the snake may then move off to another place to try again – captive snakes often become more active if they have not been fed for a number of days. The senses most used by 'sit and wait' snakes are smell, principally by means of their Jacobson's organs, and, in some boids (Plate 47) and the pit vipers, heat detection (for warm-blooded prey) via their facial pits (see pages 32–3).

In order to increase the chances of food approaching them, a number of snakes from diverse families use their tails as lures. In all of the species in

Plate 47   The heat-sensitive facial pits of pythons are clearly visible within the upper labial scales: royal python, *Python regius*.

which this behaviour has been noted, the tail is brightly coloured in yellow, white or pink and differs from the rest of the snake's body, which is usually cryptically coloured. As soon as the potential prey is noticed, the tail tip is wriggled to simulate a worm, grub or caterpillar. The prey is thus induced to investigate more closely and may even attempt to grab the 'bait', whereupon the snake strikes. One would predict that the targets of such tactics are insectivorous animals such as lizards and frogs (rather than rodents), and this appears to be the case. In fact, many large species of snakes practise tail-luring only when juvenile; as they grow, the bright colour of the tail fades, and at the same time the snake switches to larger and different prey species.

Tail-luring has been reported in (amongst others) young green tree pythons, *Chondrophython viridis*, from Papua New Guinea, Asian pit vipers of the genus *Trimeresurus* (Plate 97), and the Australian species *Acanthophis antarcticus*, which, despite its common name of death adder, is in fact a member of the cobra family. One of the Round Island boas, *Casarea dusumieri*, often lies partially buried in leaf-litter, coiled around so that the head and tail are close, but with just the tail showing. This puts it in a good position to strike if prey (lizards) approach the lure. It has been suggested that the rattle at the end of the tail of some members of the Crotalinae originally evolved as a lure, and became more specialised later, a theory which seems quite likely when one considers the large proportion of rattlesnakes which have conspicuous black and white banded tails when young.

The habit of many species which twitch their tails when stalking prey (much as a cat does) may serve to arouse the curiosity of the prey and so arrest its flight for a second or two. This behaviour may represent an intermediate stage in the evolution of tail-luring.

Other specialised hunters include those species which are largely subterranean and which seek their prey in burrows. Apart from the small rodent-eaters, such as young ratsnakes, *Elaphe* sp., and gopher snakes, *Pituophis* sp., a number of species pursue other burrowing animals through their tunnel systems, such as the *Micrurus* species mentioned above. Fish-eating snakes may peer into the water from above until a likely meal swims by, then chase it with open mouth until contact is made, but the more aquatic snakes probably employ ambush tactics much as arboreal and terrestrial species do (only beneath the surface). The strange nasal tentacles on the snout of the fishing snake, *Herpeton tentaculatum*, were at one time thought to be lures, but this theory has now fallen from favour (although no alternative explanation has been offered).

## Subduing Prey

Snakes which eat invertebrates or small and defenceless vertebrates such as fish and tadpoles merely grasp the prey in their jaws and proceed to swallow it. Their backward-pointing teeth prevent even slippery items such as frogs from escaping. The species which eat stronger, potentially harmful prey, such as other snakes, lizards, birds and mammals, kill them before swallowing, and this is achieved in one of two ways: constriction or envenomation.

The pythons and boas and many colubrid snakes constrict their prey by first grasping it in their jaws and immediately coiling a section of their body around it. By maintaining pressure with their coils, the prey is unable to draw breath and is eventually asphyxiated – the snake does not 'crush' its victim, although it is possible that a few small bones are occasionally broken. The most efficient of these constrictors can handle several mice or rats simultaneously by throwing a coil around each.

A number of species, such as the European smooth snakes, *Coronella*, and the North American indigo snake, *Drymarchon corais*, are intermediate between the straightforward swallowers and the constrictors. These snakes use their bodies to pin their prey against the ground or firm object in order to subdue it while it is being swallowed. Many species of this type feed in burrows where full-scale constriction would not be possible, but where prey can easily be crushed against the tunnel wall.

Venomous snakes can be found in three families, Colubridae, Elapidae and Viperidae, with the apparatus for injecting the venom becoming progressively more highly-developed.

The venom itself may be thought of as a modified digestive juice. In the least venomous species digestion is still its main function, whereas in the more highly-developed species its purpose is to kill prey as rapidly as possible. The composition of snake venom is extremely complex, but broadly speaking four categories are recognised.

a)  *Haemotoxins* cause a breakdown of the blood cells, leading to local bruising and internal bleeding.
b)  *Neurotoxins* affect the nervous system, especially that part controlling respiration and the heart.
c)  *Coagulants* cause clotting of the blood (thrombosis).
d)  *Anti-coagulants* prevent clotting and cause profuse bleeding.

Most venomous snakes produce a cocktail of these substances, but (very generally speaking) viper venom tends towards substances which act on the blood, whereas cobra venom affects the nervous system. Either type is equally effective on prey (and dangerous to man) but the exact toxicity of the venom from any given species will depend not only upon which substances are present, but also upon the size and state of health of the snake, the amount of venom it is carrying (i.e. when it was last used), and the nature of its prey – venoms tend to be most effective on the preferred prey of the species in question, whereas certain animals which habitually hunt snakes, for instance mongooses and king snakes, are least affected (but not totally immune).

Plate 48   *Dryophis nasuta*, a back-fanged snake, feeds mainly on arboreal lizards.

All snakes secrete saliva into their mouths, which begins the digestive process even as the prey is being swallowed – to this extent all snakes may be considered poisonous, but normally only those with specialised teeth or 'fangs' for delivering these substances are considered to be truly venomous. A number of colubrid snakes have noticeably enlarged teeth at the back of their mouths, which may be grooved, the function of which is to damage the surface of the prey and allow the venom/saliva to penetrate its bloodstream. The grooves, if present, assist the fluid to reach the site of the wound. These so-called 'back-fanged' snakes catch their prey and manipulate it as far back into their jaws as possible. By chewing on it they bring their enlarged fangs into action, and continue to hold the prey until the venom takes effect. The swallowing process then continues. Normally species of this type are not regarded as particularly dangerous to man as they have difficulty in introducing the venom unless they are able to chew their victim. A few species are large enough to be dangerous, however, and at least two of these, the boomslang, *Dispholidus typus*, and the twig snake, *Thelotornis kirtlandi* (both from Africa), have been responsible for human deaths. Other well-known back-fanged snakes (technically classed as opisthoglyphous snakes) include the black and yellow mangrove snake, *Boiga dendrophila* (Plate 86), and the long-nosed tree-snake, *Dryophis nasuta* (Plate 48), both from South-east Asia, the lyre snakes, *Trimorphodon*

83

(Plate 89) from North America, and the cat snakes, *Telescopus* (Plate 88), from southern Europe and Africa, but there are many others. None of these is likely to be very dangerous, but all back-fanged snakes should be treated with respect.

One small group of colubrids, belonging to the sub-family Aparallatinae, from Africa and the Middle East, have greatly elongated fangs at the front of the mouth, although their other teeth are few in number or absent altogether. Little is known of the method of using these fangs, which are hinged and deliver venom in much the same way as those of the vipers (see below). Because of this similarity to the true vipers (Viperidae), and their burrowing habits, these species are popularly known as 'mole vipers'.

The next stage in the development of venom apparatus (discounting the Aparallatinae, whose evolution is something of a mystery) was to shift the enlarged fangs to the front of the mouth where they could be employed more easily. All members of the Elapidae – cobras, kraits, mambas, coral snakes and sea snakes – have this arrangement and all but the very smallest are potentially dangerous to man. The cobras' feeding strategy normally consists of striking at prey, injecting the venom via the paired hollow fangs, and then holding the prey until the venom takes effect – normally quite quickly. When hunting, cobras do not spread their hood, which is a defensive behaviour pattern, as is 'spitting' in those species which are capable of it (see page 93).

The vipers are the most highly evolved of the venomous snakes, and therefore of all snakes. In these species the fangs are greatly enlarged in order to be even more effective, and to accommodate them in its mouth the snake is able, by means of a complex arrangement of bones, to fold the fangs away in the roof of its mouth when they are not required (Fig. 13). At this time they are also covered with a sheath of skin which is pulled back as the fangs are erected and the mouth opened. The gape of a large viper is such that the fangs point almost directly forward at the time of striking, the prey being 'stabbed' rather than bitten. Although vipers may hold on to small items of prey until the venom takes effect, larger morsels are bitten and immediately released. The snake then tracks down the dying animal using its tongue, until it finds the body, whereupon it is eaten. This avoids possible damage from the teeth or claws of the dying victim.

## Swallowing and Digestion

The swallowing process varies somewhat, depending on the size of the meal and whether it is alive or dead. The species which normally eat invertebrates, or snakes which feed on relatively small prey, normally grasp and swallow it without further ado. Other species which swallow their prey alive often take the trouble either to grasp it in a position which

Fig. 13  The fangs of vipers are folded away when not in use (upper) but are swung forward when the snake strikes.

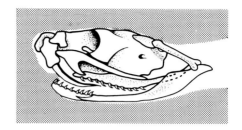

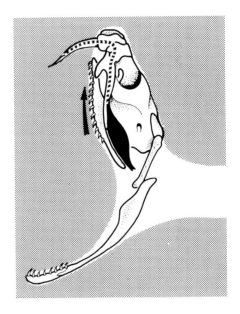

facilitates swallowing, or to work it around in their jaws until this is achieved. Normally, prey is swallowed head-first, unless it is so small that its position in the throat makes no difference.

Prey which is first killed, either by constriction or envenomation, may be closely examined for several minutes, during which time the snake continually flicks its tongue over the body, searching for the head. Once this is located, swallowing begins here, excluding the possibility of limbs or wings snagging when they reach the jaws. As the wider parts of the body enter the mouth, the bones of the lower jaw are temporarily dislocated at the points where they articulate on other bones of the head

85

(quadrate bones) and also where they join each other at the front. By this technique, snakes are able to swallow prey which is much larger than their own head, and although the capacity of large snakes is frequently exaggerated, it is certainly true that they are capable of taking remarkably large meals (Plate 49). The snake passes the prey into its gullet by alternatively moving the right and left sides of its jaws forward and pulling it in, the curved fangs acting as a series of hooks, and the flexibility of the tissue allowing irregularities to be engulfed. The whole process may take from a few seconds to several hours, although 2–5 minutes is normal. During this time the snake's mouth is completely filled and, in order to breathe, its muscular windpipe is thrust forward on the floor of its mouth and past the prey. Swallowing is completed when the prey is forced down into the stomach by rippling movements of the anterior third of the body, and may be followed by a few yawning actions as the jawbones are flexed back into their correct positions.

The process of digestion begins even before the prey reaches the snake's stomach, the saliva from its mouth and, in the case of poisonous species, the venom, acting upon it with strong enzymes. Eventually, the whole of the meal, except hair or feathers, will be digested, although this may take several days or even weeks, depending on the size of the meal and the temperature. In order to speed up the process of digestion, snakes which have recently fed bask as often as possible and, where heat is localised, they may position their stomach region in the warmest place.

Giant snakes, such as pythons, which have fed on large animals, become grotesquely distended, and have great difficulty in moving and therefore become vulnerable. For this reason, all snakes prefer to eat more moderate meals at shorter intervals, but as a last resort recently swallowed prey may be regurgitated so that the snake may escape more easily.

## Fasting

Snakes may survive without food for a considerable time, even in excess of one year under certain circumstances, although such behaviour is not normal. During hibernation, which may last for more than six months at certain latitudes, snakes do not feed, but their metabolism is greatly reduced and they may emerge weighing approximately the same as they did when they entered it. Pregnant females may be unable to feed during the latter part of pregnancy due to the space taken up by their developing eggs or young, and fasting may then occur for several months in the case of large species with long gestation periods. During this time the snake may draw upon fat laid down along each side of its spine.

The only other time that a healthy snake voluntarily shuns food is during the period prior to sloughing its skin, when its eyes are clouded over and it presumably feels vulnerable enough, without the additional burden of a stomach full of food.

Plate 49    The mouths of most snakes can accommodate large meals by means of their loosely connected bones and elastic skin: Californian kingsnake.

## Drinking

It seems likely that all snakes will drink regularly if given the chance, but many species which live in arid places can survive for months or even years without drinking, and obtain sufficient water from their food. (At the time of writing, a Californian kingsnake in my possession has remained in the best of health for two years without access to water, despite the fact that this is by no means a confirmed desert animal.) As would be expected, snakes from moist environments, for instance rain forests and stream-sides, quickly dehydrate if deprived of drinking water.

In drinking, snakes push their snouts beneath the surface and 'pump' the water into their throats by peristaltic movements of their jaws. If free-standing water is not available, they suck, rather than lap, from wet leaves and so on.

## Chapter 6
# Defence

Because all snakes are predatory animals, it is easy to overlook the fact that they are themselves preyed upon by a variety of other animals. They contribute to the diet of a large number of predatory and omnivorous birds and mammals, such as eagles, hawks, buzzards, hornbills, wild dogs and cats, hedgehogs, raccoons and badgers, which all feed on them opportunistically, but they are also systematically hunted by a number of species which specialise to some degree in eating them; for example, serpent eagles, *Circaetus* sp., roadrunners, *Geococcyx californianus*, secretary birds, *Sagittarius serpentarius*, and mongooses. All of these species and others like them are adept at locating and killing venomous, as well as harmless, snakes and may have a measure of immunity against their venom, but most rely on their speed and agility to attack and immobilise their prey before it has a chance to inflict any damage.

Like other animals, snakes 'prefer' to avoid direct confrontation, thus saving energy and eliminating the risk of injury to themselves. Their most important weapon in the armoury of self-defence, therefore, is to escape detection, and to this end most are somewhat secretive by nature. In addition, many have camouflaged or disruptive colouration, which is dealt with in Chapter 3, as is warning colouration, another, quite different means of defence. If, in spite of these devices, they are attacked, a number of behavioural defence systems may be employed, the ultimate resort (in harmless as well as venomous kinds) being to bite, often repeatedly.

## Flight

The prime objective of most snakes when attacked is to flee or seek cover as quickly as possible. Many species can move quite quickly over short distances, especially through rough terrain, and common names such as 'whipsnake' and 'racer' identify some of these. The arrangement of bands and stripes found on very many species may give the illusion of even greater speed, especially as sections of the snake appear and disappear as it travels through broken cover, such as grass and short vegetation, making it difficult for an attacker to pinpoint the snake's exact whereabouts. This represents an example of disruptive colouration allied to a fairly standard behaviour pattern. Snakes rarely stray far from cover and invariably make for a bush or pile of rocks if disturbed and it is likely that they become familiar with suitable retreats within their home range. A snake caught out in the open is at a very real disadvantage, since it can only maintain a reasonable speed over a short distance.

Plate 50   Cobras extend their hood to intimidate predators: forest cobra, *Naja melanoleuca*.

Plate 51    Hog-nosed snakes, *Heterodon* species, flatten their necks when threatened. As a last resort, they may turn over and play dead.

Plate 52 (opposite above)    *Leptophis ahaetulla*, a harmless arboreal snake from tropical America, opens its mouth widely in a threat posture.

Plate 53 (opposite below)    Ring-necked snakes, such as this *Diadophis punctatus*, raise and coil their tails to display the bright underside.

## Intimidation

After concealment or escape, the next line of defence usually consists of intimidation. This may involve expanding all, or part, of the body to increase its apparent size. The spreading hood, formed by a movement of a number of specialised ribs in the neck region, of the cobras (Plate 50) is a well-known example of this, and other snakes, such as the boomslang, *Dispholidus typus*, and the hog-nosed snakes, *Heterodon* spp. (Plate 51), inflate their throat when threatened. Alternatively, the whole body may be puffed up, as in the puff adder, *Bitis arietans*. These techniques may also involve the sudden disclosure of bright or distinctive markings on the interstitial skin, normally hidden by the overlapping scales, which may serve to startle the attacker.

Another common action is to produce an audible warning, most commonly by hissing loudly as air is expelled suddenly across a flap of skin in the throat, but also by rubbing areas of rough scales together to produce a rasping sound, as in the egg-eating snakes, *Dasypeltis* spp., or by vibrating the tail. The latter strategy is, of course, best developed in the rattlesnakes (although defence may not be the primary reason for this behaviour – see page 55). In these species, horny rings of discarded skin accumulate around the tail and produce a rapid clicking or buzzing sound when shaken, but many other species, including the rat snakes, *Elaphe* spp., also produce sound by vibrating their tails against the ground or amongst dead leaves etc.

Other means of intimidation include raising part of the body from the ground to assume a striking position; striking short of the attacker (sometimes with the mouth closed); or opening the mouth widely, in some cases to display a brightly-coloured interior, as in the aptly-named cottonmouth, *Agkistrodon piscivorus*, and the lora, *Leptophis ahaetulla* (Plate 52). Intimidation associated with colour is also found in several unrelated species with brightly coloured tails. Good examples are the Asian pipe snakes, *Cylindrophis rufus*, and the North American ringneck snakes, *Diadophis* spp. (Plate 53). These species combine a normally camouflaged dorsal surface with a warning (aposematic) colouration on the underside of their tails – when this is raised under provocation, the bright colouration may be sufficient to startle an aggressor, giving the snake time to seek cover.

## Odour

Many snakes defaecate copiously when molested, and this has been taken a stage further in a large number of colubrids which discharge a particularly pungent concoction from their anal glands and attempt to smear this over their attacker. One can only assume that the predator is put off by the thought that 'if it smells this bad, it must taste even worse'. Grass snakes, *Natrix natrix*, garter snakes, genus *Thamnophis*, kingsnakes, genus *Lampropeltis*, and the fox snake, *Elaphe vulpina* (so named for this very reason) are just a few of the many species in this category.

## Death-feigning

Following an intimidation display involving hissing and mock-striking, at least two species of harmless snakes, the European grass snake, *Natrix natrix*, and the North American hog-nosed snakes, *Heterodon* species, may turn over and pretend to be dead as a last line of defence. The effect may be enhanced by opening the mouth and allowing the tongue to hang limply. The instinct for this behaviour is so strong that, if righted, they will immediately flip back to the 'death' posture! Since many predators are quite happy to accept carrion as well as freshly-killed prey, it is difficult to assess the effectiveness of this technique, although there must be some benefit, otherwise it would not have evolved.

A slightly different strategy is employed by a few species, notably the twig snake, whereby they lie completely inert if molested, giving the impression of an inanimate object, such as a twig. This strategy, which is rare amongst snakes (but common in other animal groups such as insects), is known as *thanatosis*.

## Mimetic Behaviour

A small number of species have evolved a rather ingenious method of diverting an attack away from the most vulnerable part of their anatomy, the head. In these species, the tail, which may be coloured differently from the rest of the body, is raised and moved about in a way which simulates the movements of a snake's head – it may even appear to 'strike'. While this attracts the attention of the predator, the real head either remains hidden amongst the coils or looks around for an escape route, usually below ground or beneath a rock or log. Examples of this diverting strategy may be found amongst the burrowing boids, such as the Calabar ground python, *Calabaria reinhardtii*, the rubber boa, *Charina bottae*, and the Eurasian sand boas, such as *Eryx jaculus* (Plate 54), whose blunt tails are ideally suited to this type of deception. Its effectiveness may be gauged by the high proportion of individuals found to have scars on their tails.

## Miscellaneous Defence Strategies

Voluntary discard of a portion of the tail (caudal autotomy) is a well-known phenomenon amongst lizards but is rare in snakes. Members of at least two little-known genera (*Pliocercus* and *Scaphiodontophis*) do practise it, however.

Two African cobras, the ringhals, *Hemachatus haemachatus*, and the black-necked cobra, *Naja nigricollis*, and one Indian species, have de-

Plate 54 Several snakes, nearly all of them burrowing species, present their tail to an attacker in order to divert its attention from their head. This example, a sand boa, *Eryx jaculus*, has a number of scars on its tail to prove the effectiveness of this ploy.

veloped a means of discharging their venom which appears to be purely defensive. In these species, the ducts carrying the venom open onto the front, rather than the tip, of each fang, and by ejecting it forcibly they are able to direct a stream of venom up to 3.5 m (12 ft) with a high degree of accuracy. Any of the fluid entering the attacker's eyes will render it temporarily (or sometimes permanently) blind. Strangely, both African species seem loath to bite in the normal way in defence, although they do so when hunting, and both share with the grass snake and the hog-nosed snakes the habit of 'playing possum' as a last resort.

Finally, three species of North American snake, the coral snakes, *Micrurus fulvius* and *Micruroides euryxanthus*, and the western hook-nosed snake, *Ficimia cana*, make a popping or bubbling sound by expelling air from their vent whilst raising their tails and writhing.

# Chapter 7
# Ecology and Behaviour

All living things inter-react with their environment. Factors affecting them are of two kinds: physical (heat, light and humidity) and biological (predation, food supply and competition). Snakes obviously play their part in this system, but because most of them live out their lives in a secretive manner it can be difficult to assess their impact on the ecosystem, or its effect on them. Most observations have been made casually, frequently by non-herpetologists, and the interpretations placed on them are not necessarily accurate, and others have been made in captivity under unnatural conditions. However, in recent years a number of detailed investigations have been carried out by ecologists and be-haviouralists and preliminary results show that the lives of snakes are often far more complex and interesting than a superficial study of them would lead us to believe. Some of these investigations have brought to light aspects of snake natural history which are covered in other chapters, such as feeding, reproduction and so on, and so the purpose of this chapter will be to examine some of the more important aspects of ecology and behaviour not dealt with elsewhere.

## Thermal Ecology

All reptiles are ectotherms. This means that, unlike birds and mammals, they are incapable of producing and retaining heat within their bodies and must rely on outside sources for it. The term 'cold-blooded', often used in connection with reptiles, is not very accurate – their blood temperature obviously conforms to that of the rest of their body, which may be as warm, or warmer, than that of mammals. In fact, snakes operate most efficiently at temperatures of around 25–30°C (77–86°F) (the exact value depends on the species) and outside this preferred range their body functions slow down or stop. Each species has a critical minimum and a critical maximum temperature at which it loses the power of locomotion (and would not, therefore, be able to move to a more suitable tempera-ture). Just below and above these temperatures are the lethal minimum and lethal maximum temperatures at which the snake dies (Fig. 14).

In the tropical regions of the world the ambient temperature, both night and day, often coincides with the preferred range of snakes and so few behavioural or physiological adjustments have to be made to maintain the

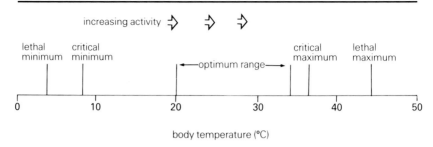

Fig. 14   Diagram showing the correlation between temperature and activity for a typical snake.

correct body temperatures. This is partly the reason why snakes are more abundant in the tropics, both in terms of numbers of individuals per unit area and also of diversity of species – for example, Trinidad, an island of only 4,800 km² (1,860 square miles), is inhabited by 37 species compared with Britain, an island of 310,000 km² (121,000 square miles), which can boast only three.

On the other hand, snakes which live in very hot places, such as deserts, need to seek protection from the sun for much of the day to prevent their bodies exceeding lethal temperature levels. Most of them are nocturnal, therefore, spending the days beneath rocks or buried in the substrate. During the hottest part of the year they may remain dormant in an underground retreat for several weeks, a process known as aestivation. Other adaptations associated with species from hot environments include pale colouration (which reflects heat) and modified scales above the eyes which probably help to reduce glare from the sun.

As we move away from the equator and the climate becomes more temperate, each individual has to spend more time and effort in raising and maintaining its body at a suitable temperature and various adaptations are seen which help to exploit the relatively small amount of available heat (the same applies to snakes living at high altitudes). Some of these adaptations concern the 'design' of the snake, whereas others affect its behaviour pattern. Thus, in cooler parts of the world, snakes tend to be smaller (less mass to warm up) and increase their surface:volume ratio by becoming stout – this cuts down on the amount of heat lost to the air. In addition, many are dark in colour, thereby increasing their absorption of radiant heat. Because of the temperature drop during the night, most temperate species are diurnal, although some of them belong to families in which the majority of species are nocturnal or crepuscular, and may have characteristics associated with this mode of life, for instance, vertical pupils.

Most temperate species bask in the sun, especially during the spring and autumn, a habit normally associated with lizards (which have slightly higher preferred body temperatures) and they may increase the efficiency of basking by flattening their body and orientating it towards the sun.

In practice, temperate species often show a shift in their activity pattern according to the time of year. In early spring they begin to emerge from their retreats around mid-morning and are active for only a few hours – on cool days they may not emerge at all. As the weather improves they gradually begin to emerge earlier and retreat later until, at the height of summer, they may need to seek shelter during the hottest part of the day. As the days become shorter and cooler again in the autumn, activity is once more restricted to the middle of the day until eventually the snakes are unable to raise their temperatures sufficiently to become active and hibernation takes place.

Immediately prior to this they seek out underground retreats (hibernacula) where they will be protected from lethally low temperatures. In extreme cases, they may spend more than half of each year in a state of torpor, leaving only a few months in which to build up food reserves and reproduce. Reproduction itself then becomes a problem because the long incubation period required for snake eggs to develop means that the young will not hatch before winter sets in. One method of avoiding this is to retain the eggs in the body of the female so that she can speed up their development by raising her own body temperature by basking. In this way the young are born at the end of the summer and can begin feeding before they are forced to hibernate. Unfortunately, this also means that the female will be very short of food, having fasted during the latter part of pregnancy due to the increasing amount of space occupied by the developing embryos. The results of this 'trade-off' between the well-being of the mother and her offspring are that snakes living at the extremes of their temperature tolerance only reproduce every two or three years, the barren years being used to make good the food reserves which were depleted during the reproductive year. An alternative strategy is to lay the eggs amongst rotting vegetation, where the heat produced by the processes of decomposition will speed up their development – the European grass snake, *Natrix natrix*, is a well-known exponent of this technique and there are undoubtedly many others.

## Water Balance

The reptiles' ability to conserve water and move into dry habitats was one of the most important factors in the evolution of the vertebrates. The scaly skin of snakes, when compared to that of their ancestors, the amphibians, obviously retains water quite efficiently, but is not totally impervious. More importantly, they are able to re-cycle a large proportion of the water in their urinary system and excrete nitrogenous waste material in a semi-solid form (as uric acid crystals, a white substance requiring only a little water to carry it out of the body). As is to be expected, those species which live in arid regions are far more resistant to dehydration than those from moist habitats such as swamps and tropical rain forests.

## Salt Balance

A small number of aquatic snakes live habitually or occasionally in salt or brackish water. These species are primarily the sea snakes, but also include the wart snakes (Acrochordidae) and certain colubrids belonging to the sub-family Homolopsinae. All of these species have a common problem to overcome: they must extract the surplus salt from their bodies without the benefit of fresh drinking water with which to flush their systems. In the sea snakes and wart snakes this is achieved by means of a specialised salt-secreting gland at the base of their tongue (the sub-lingual gland) which collects salt water via the tubular sheath around the tongue, which then pushes the salty water out each time it is extended. The colubrids which enter brackish water do not possess this gland and it is assumed that they are able to maintain their water balance because of the relatively low salinity of their habitat and by drinking only the fresh water which collects on leaves etc following rain. Perhaps more importantly, they obtain much of their water from their food.

## Population Ecology

Population ecology is concerned with relationships between individuals of the same species, a population being a group of animals of the same species living in the same area. This population should consist of adults of both sexes, sub-adults and juveniles. If the population is expanding there will be a large number of juveniles, but if it is dying out it will consist mainly of adults. The limited number of snake populations which have been studied appear to show fairly stable levels; in other words, the proportions of these three age classes do not vary greatly from year to year, but exact figures are difficult to obtain owing to the secretive nature of the animals, especially when young, and the problems associated with sampling the types of habitats involved. The results of these surveys also show, amongst other things, that the ratio of males to females is roughly equal, and that migration of animals into and out of the population is limited. Mortality is much higher in younger animals than adults, and once animals reach reproductive size they are relatively long-lived. (Growth-rates, reproductive success and home-ranges can all be established for every individual within the colony by marking each animal when it is first caught – subsequent captures then provide such data as length, weight and location. Over a period of several years a fairly accurate picture can be built up of the population's characteristics.)

The most thorough studies of snake populations include those of the adder, *Vipera berus*, in southern England, the copperhead, *Agkistrodon contortrix*, in Kansas, and the black rat snake, *Elaphe obsoleta*, also in Kansas. Unfortunately, such a small number of species have been studied that it is dangerous to assume that all snake populations work in the same way. Moreover, there have been no detailed studies of rain forest species, aquatic species, any of the 'giant' snakes, or any of the small burrowing species. The opportunities for research in this field are enormous.

## Community Ecology

Community ecology is concerned with relationships with other species. All snakes share their environment with other organisms – plants and animals. Many members of this community have little or no bearing on the snakes, but others control to a large extent their well-being or otherwise. These fall into a number of categories: prey species; predators; competitors; parasites. Some may be in more than one of these categories: for example, young birds or eggs may form part of the prey of a particular snake, whereas the adults, if carnivorous, may compete with the same species for food, or may even prey upon it.

Food has already been discussed at some length in Chapter 5 with the conclusion that, although some species are very specialised in their dietary requirements, others are more opportunistic, taking more or less any prey of suitable size when it is available. When food is abundant, the relevant population(s) of snakes would be expected to expand, and during a scarcity of prey the numbers will decline, but as snakes are able to fast for long periods of time they are not as dependent on a constant food supply as many other predators, and populations tend, therefore, to be relatively stable. Food shortage can have serious repercussions, however, on very young snakes, particularly those of temperate species which are born or hatch in late summer and must accumulate food reserves quickly in order to hibernate successfully. In extreme cases, almost all of a single year's hatchlings may perish.

Young snakes are also more prone to predation by a variety of animals because they are more easily overpowered by a greater number of predators than their adult counterparts, and also because they are less experienced at avoiding them. This, of course, is the reason why each female produces far more eggs or young during her reproductive life than are needed to replace adults which die – the vast majority of her young will either starve or be killed before they reach sexual maturity. The effects of natural predation on a population are not normally serious – as the population density is reduced, the predator(s) will move to another area or another prey, giving the original population a chance to recover. In this way, a balance is achieved between the snake population (as prey) and its predators, as well as between the snake population (as predators) and its prey.

Plate 55 The smooth snake, *Coronella austriaca*, is found in northern Europe and at high altitudes in the south.

Competitors of snakes are mainly those which compete for food as opposed to territory. In practice, snakes are so highly skilled in seeking out and killing prey that their competitors are few, and consist of birds, small carnivorous mammals and snakes of other species with similar food preferences (if present). The members of animal communities rarely compete vigorously for a resource: during the course of evolution the less successful species are eliminated and those which remain are normally the most efficient exploiters of their own 'niche'. The two species of smooth snakes (genus *Coronella*) which inhabit Europe illustrate this point nicely. Both are roughly the same size (to about 60 cm, 2 ft) and both eat lizards and small rodents. Were they to occur together in the same area they would doubtless compete, but in fact *Coronella austriaca* (Plate 55) occupies cooler regions in northern and central Europe (and high ground in the south), whereas the other species, *C. girondica* (Plate 56), is more southern in distribution. It is doubtful if *C. austriaca* 'prefers' lower temperatures, but it is likely that it has been ousted from the warmer areas because *C. girondica* is more efficient in some way or other.

Conversely, if the snake fauna within a given area is tabulated it will usually be found that each species differs from the others in such factors as

Plate 56    The southern smooth snake, *Coronella girondica*, is restricted to low and moderate altitudes in southern Europe.

habitat, food preference, activity pattern or size, so avoiding direct competition. This sharing of an area is known as 'resource partitioning'. The artificial introduction of other predators, such as domestic cats, to an area, however, often tilts the balance and the original inhabitants, including snakes, quickly decline in numbers and may eventually become extinct.

Most wild snakes carry some degree of parasite burden. These parasites include ticks and mites (ectoparasites), and flukes, roundworms, tape-worms and protozoans (endoparasites). Since it is the hallmark of a successful parasite to exploit its host without killing it, few of these seriously affect the health of the snake unless it is under some additional stress (e.g. in captivity). Furthermore, many of the endoparasites are host-specific, that is to say that each species of snake has a set of parasites peculiar to it, although closely related species may share certain parasite species. Infestation by endoparasites normally occurs via the snake's food, and most parasites lead double lives – one stage inhabits a prey animal, such as a fish, and the other stage inhabits the snake which preys upon that fish. If the snake plays host to the reproductive stage of the parasite then it will excrete its eggs, some of which will find their way back to another fish, so completing the cycle.

Ticks and mites are not transmitted in this way, nor are they totally host-specific. They may be spread by direct contact between snakes, perhaps when they come together to hibernate, or they may leave their host and live in the ground or amongst vegetation until another snake passes by. The process of skin-sloughing may temporarily rid the snake of its ectoparasites.

In a parasite-host relationship, the parasite is the only species to gain any benefit, but under certain circumstances the host may also benefit in some way. Examples of this 'mutualism' are not easily found amongst snakes, but the back of the fishing snake, *Erpeton tentaculatum* (Plate 19), frequently becomes covered with algae – in this way, the snake provides a surface for the algae to grow on, and at the same time the algae enhance the snake's camouflage.

## Habitats

A wide variety of habitats are utilised by snakes, some more so than others. Although many species are not restricted to one particular type, most have their preferences and some are strictly limited.

Plate 57    Montane rain forest, Trinidad. A number of terrestrial and arboreal species inhabit this type of habitat.

Plate 58   Desert, Arizona. Snakes are amongst the most successful colonisers of deserts in many parts of the world.

### 1)   Forests

Temperate forests are not very suitable for snakes because the sun rarely penetrates the canopy and the forest floor is therefore usually cool. A small number of species may be found on the fringes of forests, or in clearings and at the sides of paths and tracks. In this way they are able to bask, and also benefit from the ample cover and from an abundant food supply in the form of rodents, birds and lizards.

Tropical forests, on the other hand, are often incredibly rich in species (Plate 57). Temperature is not a problem and a wide variety of habitats are available: the various canopy layers are inhabited by arboreal species; the forest floor has its population of terrestrial species; and burrowing species live in the leaf-litter and below. Observing snakes in this type of habitat can be exceedingly difficult – the availability of plenty of cover, the camouflaged markings of many tropical forest species and the fact that they rarely bask in the open combine to make this community one of the least known, and many species are undoubtedly yet to be discovered. They have a huge variety of prey on which to feed, ranging from invertebrates through amphibians, other reptiles, birds and mammals. Of the eleven families of snakes, only one (the aquatic wart snakes, Acrochordidae) is not represented in tropical forests in some part of the world.

## 2) Deserts

Snakes, along with their close relatives, the lizards, are amongst the most successful colonisers of the world's deserts — their relatively impermeable skin and the ability to conserve water by excreting uric acid as a solid obviously have advantages in dry environments (Plate 58). Most desert species are active at night or during the early morning/late evening, and prey on lizards and small mammals.

Several desert species are able to move across loose sand by 'sidewinding' (see page 29) and many burrow into it to escape from intense heat and/or to conceal themselves from predators and prey. Desert species are found amongst the Boidae, Colubridae, Elapidae and, especially, the Viperidae.

## 3) Mountains

Montane environments present a serious problem to snakes: that of temperature extremes, both on a daily and a seasonal scale. In the tropics, many mountains are cloaked in forests which 'buffer' the two extremes, but high mountain ranges, especially in temperate regions, are not heavily populated by snakes (Plate 59). Vipers have moved into this niche to a greater extent than other families — the Himalayan pit viper, *Agkistrodon himalayanus*, has been found at greater altitudes (4,900 m, 16,000 ft) than any other snake; a number of small rattlesnakes, for instance the ridge-nosed rattlesnake, *Crotalus willardi*, are found at altitudes of over 4,000 m (13,000 ft) in Mexico; and in Europe three species of vipers (*Vipera berus*, *V. aspis* and *V. ursinii*) occur up to about 3,000 m (10,000 ft) in the Alps.

Plate 59   Dolomite mountains, Italy. Seasonal and diurnal extremes of temperature limit the number of species found in the mountains of temperate parts of the world.

Plate 60    Oropouche River, Trinidad. Large numbers of aquatic, semi-aquatic and moisture-loving species occur in and around tropical lakes and streams.

## 4) Rivers and Lakes

Most snakes can swim and may do so when moving from one area to another or if flooding occurs, but some are almost totally aquatic. Most of these are tropical in distribution and all feed on other aquatic creatures, such as fish and amphibian larvae. True water snakes belong to two families, the Colubridae and the Acrochordidae, but a few snakes from other families (Boidae, Elapidae and Viperidae) are semi-aquatic in habit and these may be found in marsh or swamp regions, or along riversides in temperate as well as tropical parts of the world (Plate 60), feeding on fish, amphibians, reptiles and mammals which either inhabit the water permanently or visit it in order to drink, breed etc. Some of these species may have morphological modifications associated with their way of life, such as a tail which is flattened from side to side and upward-pointing eyes and nostrils.

## 5) The Sea

Only one group of snakes has successfully overcome the problems associated with a completely marine existence. These are the sea snakes, comprising two sub-families of the cobra family, the Hydrophinae and the Laticaudinae. These species spend their entire lives in warm tropical seas (Plate 61), although the latter must go ashore to lay its eggs (the Hydrophinae are ovo-viviparous). All sea snakes are fish-eaters. A single member of the Acrochordidae (*A. granulatus*) occurs in coastal waters, and another species (*A. javanicus*) occasionally enters estuaries. Both of these species, like the sea snakes, eat fish.

Plate 61   The open sea – only the sea snakes, Hydrophinae, have colonised the oceans, and then only in tropical parts.

Plate 62   Mediterranean scrub, Spain. Large-scale land clearance over many centuries has produced a semi-natural landscape which may suit certain snakes, such as the whipsnakes, genus *Coluber*.

## 6)   Man-made Habitats

Man's modifications to the earth's surface are plain to see. In general, his activities are injurious to wildlife, but a few species, including some snakes, have adapted to the artificial habitats so created. Agricultural regions are often inhabited by rodent-eating species, some of which may also prey upon chickens etc. The large-scale clearing of woodland, and subsequent reversion to scrub, as in the Mediterranean region (Plate 62), actually encourages colonisation by species which require open spaces, whereas city parks and gardens may provide good hunting ground for small, secretive, insectivorous snakes. Unfortunately, these are isolated cases and in no way compensate for the loss of natural habitats.

## Patterns of Distribution

On looking at the distribution maps of the eleven families of snakes (Chapter 9), it soon becomes clear that some families are far more widespread than others, and that some areas are inhabited by a number of families, some by only a few, and some by none at all. Part of the reason for this discrepancy can be attributed to suitable or unsuitable climates and habitats, but superimposed on this picture is that of the geological history of the world, particularly the sequence of events taking place around the Mesozoic era when the various land masses broke up and drifted apart, forming barriers in the shape of oceans which snakes were unable to cross, thus limiting, to a large extent, each family to the area over which it had already spread. Between that time and the present, many species, and indeed whole families, have undoubtedly become extinct for a variety of reasons, leaving a pattern of distribution which is not always easy to explain or understand (particularly as fossil records of snakes and their ancestors are so rarely discovered).

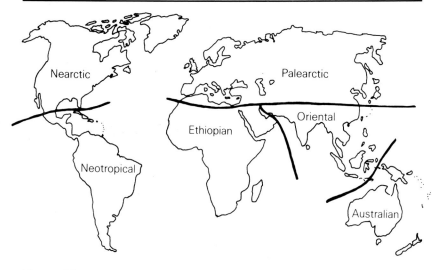

Map 1    The zoogeographical regions of the world.

It is useful, however, to look at the main zoogeographical regions of the world (Map 1) and discuss the 'quota' of snake species and families found in each and to try to postulate the reasons behind these occurrences and absences.

## 1)    Nearctic (North America)

The main elements here are a large number of colubrids, showing wide diversity (burrowing, terrestrial, semi-arboreal and semi-aquatic). Viperids are also well represented, but only by the sub-family Crotalinae (pit vipers), mainly the rattlesnakes, *Crotalus* and *Sistrurus* species. Additional elements comprise 2 species of leptotyphlopids, 3 or 4 species of boids and a small number of elapids (coral snakes only). These mainly tropical families range into the most southerly, and therefore warmer, parts of this region.

Total – 5 families (none endemic).

## 2)    Neotropical (Central and South America)

Primitive burrowing snakes are well represented by members of the families Leptotyphlopidae, Typhlopidae and Anomalepidae, the latter being unique (endemic) to this region. There is also a great diversity of boids and colubrids, and the Elapidae is represented by a number of species of coral snakes and the Viperidae by many pit vipers, including rattlesnakes and several other genera.

A false coral snake, *Anilius scytale*, which, for the time being at least, is classified with the pipe snakes (Aniliidae), a predominantly Asian family, has a wide range over much of tropical South America.

Total – 6 families (1 endemic).

### 3)  Palearctic (Europe and Northern Asia, extreme North Africa)

Large numbers of colubrids and viperids (including members of both sub-families) occur. In addition, small numbers of snakes belonging to the families Typhlopidae, Leptotyphlopidae, Boidae and Elapidae are found, mainly in the warmer regions towards the south of this region.

Total – 6 families (none endemic).

### 4)  Ethiopian (Africa, excepting the Mediterranean coastal region)

Six families all occur in fairly large numbers: Typhlopidae, Leptotyphlopidae, Boidae, Colubridae, Elapidae and Viperidae (only the true vipers, sub-family Viperinae). A great diversity of habitats has given rise to a number of specialised forms within the last four of these families, including burrowing, terrestrial, arboreal and aquatic species.

Total – 6 families (none endemic).

N.B. Madagascar is unusual in that it is thought to have broken away from the African mainland before that became detached from the South American land mass. Its fauna therefore consists of groups of animals which were later superseded on the African mainland by more advanced forms, but which survived on Madagascar through lack of competition. Its snake fauna consists of three families: Typhlopidae, Boidae and Colubridae. Of special interest are the boas, of which the three species found here are more closely related to South American species than to their closest neighbours in Africa.

### 5)  Oriental (South and South-east Asia)

This region appears to have been the centre of evolution for a number of families of snakes and contains many interesting elements. Apart from having given rise to a large number of specialised sub-families of colubrids, the ubiquitous families Typhlopidae, Boidae, Elapidae (all three sub-families) and Viperidae (all three sub-families) are well represented.

In addition, the Acrochordidae has the majority of its range within this region, the Uropeltidae is found only in a small portion of the Indian sub-continent, the Aniliidae is endemic but for a single (somewhat dubious) member in South America, and the single species belonging to the family Xenopeltidae is found here.

Total – 9 families (2 endemic).

6) Australian (New Guinea, Australia and New Zealand)

The Typhlopidae, Boidae and Elapidae are all well represented. There are few colubrids (and those only in the north) and no viperids. This, being the last family to have evolved, must have appeared on the scene too late to have crossed over from South-east Asia. The elapids (Australia's most numerous family) have therefore diversified remarkably to fill the niches normally occupied by vipers and colubrids, and two of these (genus *Acanthophis*) are so viper-like in appearance that they are commonly referred to by the misleading name of 'death adders'. The Acrochordidae occur around Australia's northern coast and enter several river systems in this region.

Total – 5 families (none endemic).

N.B. New Zealand has no snakes at all: although it was originally part of the land mass which broke away with Australia, it is presumed to have sunk at some time during its history, and then re-emerged. Its fauna therefore consists only of species which have arrived in the same way that oceanic islands were colonised, i.e. by flying or rafting – snakes rarely indulge in either of these activities.

# Chapter 8
# Snakes and Man

The extent to which snakes have figured in the history of many civilisations is out of all proportion to their economic importance. They first appear in cave paintings in France and Spain alongside bison and other food animals, and from that era right through until the present day we can find evidence of man's obsession with them as symbols of good, evil, healing, fertility, immortality and superstition. A complete account of the inter-relationship between mankind and snakes would be a full-scale anthropological exercise – here it will be sufficient to mention some of the more important, interesting and bizarre aspects of the association.

## Snake Worship

Snake worship has existed in many widely scattered parts of the world, often seeming to have arisen independently in many cultures.

In Australia, snakes feature in several aboriginal myths and legends and are especially associated with rain and thus with the creation of life. The 'ungud' or rainbow serpent lives in water-holes which it guards and prevents from drying up. In return for these services, ceremonies involving the restoration of its image on cave walls must be performed at the beginning of each rainy season. In central Australia, a similar creature is known as 'yarapi', a serpent of enormous proportions, whose tail always rests in an important water-hole.

Python worship was common amongst tribes in central Africa and killing a python was regarded as a serious crime, punishable by death. From here, slaves took their religion to the West Indies, especially to Haiti, where it is still (surreptitiously) practised under the name of voodoo.

In India, cobras were believed to be reincarnations of important chiefs and were known as 'nagas' (female versions were known as 'naginis'). They controlled rain and other factors affecting the villagers' well-being and were feared as well as worshipped for their ability to bring disaster and benefit alike. In other parts of Asia, snakes were thought of as fertility symbols and in Japan the god of thunder was portrayed as a snake.

Their association with rain and fertility is found again in North and Central America, where many Indian tribes, in common with the Aztecs and the Mayas, revered the snake. The most famous ceremonies are probably those of the Hopi Indians in New Mexico. These people look upon the snakes as messengers to the rain gods and after performing rituals and dances with the animals they release them near holes and fissures in the ground to make their way to the underworld with the Indians' wishes. These ceremonies still take place, but have apparently become somewhat tainted with commercialism in recent years.

In the Mediterranean region snakes were widely worshipped, especially by the ancient Egyptians who identified them with the River Nile, and therefore with fertility, and a rearing cobra was incorporated into the head-dress of the Pharaoh. The Greeks, on the other hand, regarded the snake as a symbol of reincarnation and healing, owing to its ability to slough off its old skin and reappear brighter and healthier. The god of medicine, Askelepios (latinised to Aesculapius) was originally identified as a snake and in later times, when he took on a human form, a snake appeared in his motif, variations of which, known as a cauduceus, have been adopted by numerous branches of the medical profession. Both the Greeks and the Romans encouraged snakes to take up residence around their homes and temples, and even introduced snakes into parts of their empire. (This may account for the fragmented distribution of the Aesculapian snake, *Elaphe longissima*, one of their most 'popular' species.)

Christianity has not treated the snake so kindly. The exact interpretation of the Garden of Eden episode is widely disputed but its effect has been to portray the snake as an evil influence. Even so, snake festivals still occur, for instance in the village of Cucullo in central Italy, where snakes are collected by villagers and paraded through the streets during May, accompanied by a statue of St Dominic of Folingo. Former times saw the snakes killed and buried after the ceremony and this allegedly protected the villagers from snakebite (and toothache!), but now the snakes, consisting mainly of *Elaphe longissima*, *E. quatuorlineata* and *Coluber viridiflavus*, are sold to tourists and collectors once the festival is over.

In the early part of this century a snake-handling cult arose in the United States, the members of which freely handled rattlesnakes, believing that their faith would protect them from being bitten. In the event of an 'accident' they relied on prayer alone to bring about recovery. Not surprisingly, several came to a sticky end (including one George Hensley, founder of the cult) and the ceremonies were eventually outlawed in most states.

## Man versus Snakes

Snakes have been, and still are, exploited in a number of ways. The flesh of a variety of species has been claimed to be effective in curing or preventing almost every disease known to man. In the Orient, the Chinese ate them as a cure for tuberculosis, and sea snakes were considered effective against malaria, epilepsy and other diseases. Venom was valued as a cure for cholera, dysentery, meningitis and gangrene in various parts of the world, and although its usefulness against these ailments is dubious to say the least, dried Russell's viper venom has been widely used as a blood coagulant in recent years, although it has gradually been replaced by other, less costly, drugs.

Strangely, snakes are not much eaten as an item of diet, probably due to the superstitions and taboos which stem from religious and other beliefs, but they are important to some groups of Australian aborigines who eat them out of necessity; to certain communities in Japan, China and Hong Kong, to whom they are a delicacy; and to a small number of people in North America, who eat rattlesnake flesh out of curiosity.

The skins of snakes, particularly the larger species, are used in the manufacture of clothes, bags, shoes and musical instruments, although the popularity of these goods waxes and wanes with fashion (Plate 63). Certain species are especially valuable in this respect, notably the wart snake, *Acrochordus javanicus*, whose warty scales can be crushed to produce a skin of uniform appearance, known as 'karung'. Other species which are sought for their skins are large boas and pythons and two large Asian ratsnakes, *Ptyas korros* and *P. mucosus*.

In the field of entertainment, the use of snakes by snake-charmers of North Africa and India is the example which springs most readily to mind. This profession has existed for many generations and much mystery

Plate 63  Snakeskin products, an up-market fashion, result in the deaths of thousands of snakes, mainly Asian, each year.

surrounds the techniques involved. The favoured species for this kind of display are cobras, the most instantly recognisable of dangerous snakes, and especially (in the areas where they occur) the king cobra or hamadryad, *Ophiophagus hannah*. Although some performers 'cheat' by sewing up the mouths of their snakes, pulling their fangs, or cutting the venom ducts, the majority work with intact animals and rely on their knowledge of the snakes' behaviour to avoid accidents. Some do get bitten, sometimes fatally, and this is regarded as an occupational hazard. In North America, roadside rattlesnake shows used to be a common feature of desert regions, and very large or allegedly dangerous specimens may be exhibited in circuses or fairground sideshows.

Most zoos exhibit snakes, sometimes a few of the more spectacular species, sometimes a representative collection of local or foreign species. All too often snakes are displayed as curiosities, but a small number of these zoos specialise in snakes and other reptiles and the breeding results from some of them are admirable. Snake parks exist in some tropical and subtropical countries and they may participate actively in the collection of venom, herpetological research, and education, as well as providing entertainment for the general public. In addition to the demand for zoos and snake parks, there is a steady trade in snakes destined for a growing number of private collectors who keep snakes and other reptiles, due either to a leaning toward more bizarre 'pets', or to a serious interest in this group of animals.

The animals may be obtained locally, often by the simple expedient of offering a reward for the required species, although the collection of the rarer or more secretive kinds necessitates considerable specialised know-ledge of their habitat preferences and activity patterns. In the warmer parts of the world, a well-tried method of collecting snakes or sampling an area is to drive slowly at night along tarmac or concrete roads passing through deserts, rainforests or other good snake country. Snakes which cross these roads during the course of their nocturnal perambulations often linger on them for a while, enjoying the warmth which they retain, but sacrificing the benefits of cryptic colouration, and are easily picked out in the headlights. Stopping the car and leaping out to bag the snake before it disappears into the surrounding countryside requires quick reflexes and a certain agility, but the results often exceed those obtained by more conventional (but strenuous) techniques.

Commercial sources of snakes are concentrated in countries where snakes are not only common, but also enjoy little or no protection in the form of laws regulating their collection and exportation. Large-scale snake dealing is carried out in parts of South-east Asia, especially Thailand, where the 'harvesting' of local flora and fauna is an accepted means of earning a living. Unfortunately, despite the quite high prices of snakes at retail outlets, their value at source is small, leading to a complete lack of concern for their health and survival rate. Large numbers of animals are

Plate 64   The common boa epitomises the large constricting snakes and is a popular 'pet'.

held in inadequate accommodation prior to shipment, causing stress, disease, and consequently high mortality. The problem is compounded by the continual demand for species which have highly specialised requirements or a restricted diet (or both) and for which the life expectancy under even the best of captive conditions is extremely short. A prime example of these high-demand, low-survival species is the long-nosed tree-snake, *Dryophis nasuta* (Plate 14), a beautiful and interesting species which requires a constant diet of small lizards in order to thrive. Yet another problem is the availability of large numbers of young pythons, especially the reticulated python, *P. reticulatus*, a species which adapts quite well to captivity but which grows to a potential 9 or 10 metres (30–33 ft).

After South-east Asia, the most important centre for snake dealing is probably North America, which acts as a distribution centre for Central and South American species, e.g. *Boa constrictor* (Plate 64), as well as for its native species, especially garter snakes, *Thamnophis* spp. (Plate 65), ratsnakes, *Elaphe* spp., and kingsnakes, *Lampropeltis* spp.

Owing to the growing popularity of snake-keeping as a hobby, they are now becoming big business, an ominous situation, not only for the animals themselves, but also for the serious enthusiasts who are now

Plate 65   The common garter snake, *Thamnophis sirtalis* – thousands find their way into pet shops.

finding it increasingly difficult to locate reliable sources of legally obtained healthy animals. The commercial exploitation of any snakes, even common species, on a large scale, is deplorable but, despite the misgivings over this trade, the numbers involved are probably insignificant when compared to other effects, for example habitat destruction. Furthermore, there is little demand for rarities, and many of the more desirable species are now being successfully bred in captivity, a pursuit which not only reduces the pressure on wild populations, but which also promotes the development of techniques which may well be instrumental in saving endangered species in years to come.

Explicit instructions for maintaining and breeding snakes must be sought elsewhere, but their basic requirements are a warm (20–25°C, 68–77°F), dry vivarium, which is well ventilated, furnished with a suitable hiding place and a water dish. The substrate may be newspaper, bark chippings, wood shavings or peagravel, and the natural habits of the species concerned should be taken into account, e.g. arboreal species should be given a tall vivarium with branches on which to climb. Food of the correct type should be supplied regularly and precautions should be taken to ensure that cross-infection from newly-acquired, and therefore potentially diseased, specimens does not occur. Captive-bred animals are always preferable to wild, imported stock, even though they may be slightly more expensive, and these are readily obtained by joining a society whose members specialise in keeping reptiles. If it is hoped to breed from the animals, it may be necessary to manipulate certain of the environmental parameters, such as temperature, daylength and humidity to simulate natural seasonal changes, and some experimentation in this field may be necessary before interesting things start to occur.

Generally speaking, snakes can be the easiest of animals to care for successfully once a grasp of their basic requirements has been obtained, but as they are not capable of showing gratitude or affection, they are suitable only for those persons who have a genuine interest in them and who are prepared to dedicate time, effort and money to their maintenance.

Although the outlook for snakes which are collected for zoos or the pet trade may not be too bright, it is decidedly gloomy for those that are collected for museums, because the greater majority of these specimens are destined to inhabit jars of formalin or other preservative, where they may form part of a reference collection with which other specimens can be compared for identification and classification. Alternatively, they may be dissected in order that the size, shape and position of their internal working parts can be investigated. Fortunately, the inclusion of a snake dissection on teaching syllabuses has now been largely abandoned – more through economic reasons than through concern for their continuing survival.

## Snakes versus Man

The ability of snakes to kill humans has contributed not only to their persecution but also to their exploitation by venom institutes who require large numbers of poisonous snakes to produce the antidote, known as antivenin, to their bite. This is achieved by first 'milking' the snake by encouraging it to squirt its venom into a glass vessel and then injecting a large animal, usually a horse, with a series of sub-lethal doses of the venom until immunity is built up. Its serum is then extracted and purified and this substance becomes the antivenin. Unfortunately, the composition of venoms varies greatly from species to species and so a wide range of antivenins is necessary for complete protection (and the culprit must be correctly identified), although antivenin 'cocktails' or polyvalent antivenins are produced which give protection against a range of species, usually those living in a particular country or region (Plate 66).

Deaths from snake-bite are obviously more frequent where venomous species are more common, but also depend on other factors such as the density of the human population and the proportion of these who work on the land, whether or not the wearing of shoes is practised, and the availability of medical facilities (and the willingness of the people to use them). The incidence of death from snake-bite *per capita* is highest in the

117

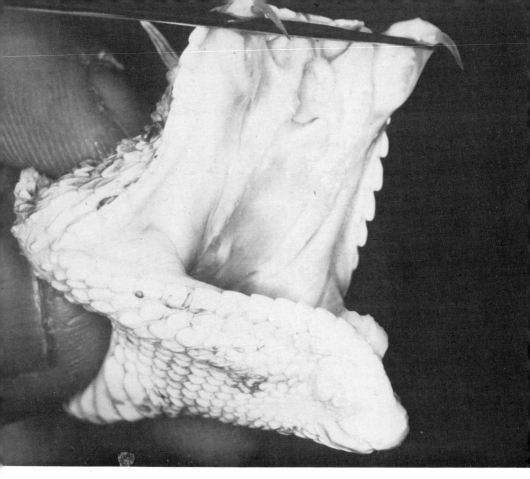

Plate 66    The fangs of a horned viper, *Cerastes cerastes*, from which a yellow fluid (venom) is secreted.

Indian sub-continent (Burma, India and Sri Lanka) and in parts of North Africa and South America.

The World Health Organisation has estimated the number of fatal snake-bites in India at 10,000 to 12,000 *per annum*, about 0.005 per cent of the population. In Burma, the total number of deaths is smaller (about 2,000), but this represents 0.015 per cent of the much smaller population, and Sri Lanka and the Philippines have slightly lower figures. The main culprits in these countries are the Indian cobra, *Naja naja*, Russell's viper, *Vipera russelli* and the saw-scaled viper, *Echis carinatus*. The places with the highest incidence of bites, however, are certain islands of the Ryukyu group, between Japan and Taiwan, where about 0.2 per cent of the population suffer bites every year, mostly due to the habu, *Trimeresurus flavoviridis*, but as this is not a particularly deadly snake the vast majority of victims recover.

In South America, about 2,000 deaths are attributed to snake-bite each

Plate 67   *Bothrops atrox*, the most widespread and dangerous of South and Central America's venomous snakes.

year, of which the pit viper, *Bothrops atrox* (Plate 67), is responsible for about one third. The remainder are caused by other *Bothrops* species, a rattlesnake, *Crotalus durissus*, and coral snakes, *Micrurus* species. In Africa, the puff adder, *Bitis arientans*, Egyptian cobra, *Naja haje*, and the saw-scaled viper cause about 1,000 deaths per year.

All of these 'high-risk' areas are notably poor in terms of medical facilities and their populations consist largely of peasant farmers. By comparison, Australia, with its abundance of venomous species, suffers only 5–10 deaths *per annum*, mainly through the tiger snake, *Notechis scutatus*, and the brown snake, *Pseudonaja textilis*; the United States has about 15 mortalities, mainly from the eastern and western diamondback rattlesnakes, *Crotalus adamanteus* and *C. atrox*; and less than 15 people die in the whole of Europe (mainly in the south-eastern countries where the sand viper, *Viper ammodytes*, occurs). The low casualty rate in Europe and the United States could undoubtedly be reduced still further if encounters with venomous snakes were not treated as opportunities to display bravado by exhibitionists and would-be heroes!

It is of interest that the largest and therefore potentially the most dangerous species of venomous snakes account for very few deaths. The reason is that these animals, listed below, are not often encountered, either because they are restricted to remote and thinly populated regions, or because they are, on the whole, shy and retiring.

The six largest species of venomous snakes are found scattered throughout the world:

| | | |
|---|---|---|
| King cobra, *Ophiophagus hannah* | Asia | to 4.8 m (16 ft) |
| Black mamba, *Dendroaspis polylepis* | Africa | to 4.3 m (14 ft) |
| Taipan, *Oxyuranus scutellatus* | Australia | to 4 m (13 ft) |
| Bushmaster, *Lachesis muta* | S. America | to 3 m (10 ft) |
| Eastern diamondback rattlesnake, *Crotalus adamanteus* | N. America | to 2.4 m (8 ft) |
| Gaboon viper, *Bitis gabonica* | Africa | to 1.8 m (6 ft) |

Note that the first three are elapids and of slender build (Plate 68), whereas the other three are vipers and therefore heavy-bodied, especially the gaboon viper.

Two important factors when assessing the relative danger of bites from the various species are the amount of venom each produces, and its

Plate 68 The black mamba, *Dendroaspis polylepis*, amongst the most feared of African snakes.

potency. Size for size, vipers tend to give higher yields of venom than elapids, with the gaboon viper head of the list, closely followed by the bushmaster and several of the larger rattlesnakes. However, where potency is concerned, the cobra family has few equals, especially the sea snakes, sub-family Hydrophinae, some of which produce venom which is nearly one hundred times more effective than that of the gaboon viper. Other highly potent venoms are those used by the kraits, genus *Bungarus*, and four Australian species, the taipan, the inland taipan, the brown snake and the tiger snake. Of the vipers, the saw-scaled viper, *Echis carinatus*, probably has the most powerful venom. This, combined with its small size, habit of lying buried in sand, and irascibility, probably make it the world's most dangerous snake.

It would be unfair to leave this section without mentioning the other side of the coin, i.e. the ways in which mankind may benefit from snakes (although it should not be considered essential that any group of animals is beneficial to us in order to argue for its protection and preservation).

There can be no doubt that snakes are of enormous benefit to agricultural communities, although this fact is rarely recognised, and harmless as well as venomous kinds are still persecuted almost universally. There are parts of the world, however, where pythons and other large snakes are tolerated and even encouraged to take up residence in grain-stores and barns. The extent to which they control rodent pests is obviously difficult to estimate, but their efficiency as hunters and killers, coupled with their ability to enter burrows and nests in order to take young mice and rats is significant. A number of species, such as the North American indigo snake and king snakes, specialise in hunting their venomous 'relatives' and this may endear them to us, although they can hardly be said to be acting out of any feelings of altruism towards man – all will take non-venomous kinds with equal enthusiasm.

Their most important contribution is in belonging to the overall structure of an environment to which we all belong, and any attempt to remove them from that structure could be compared to the removal of a single brick from a building – its effect may not be immediately obvious, but the long-term consequences would almost certainly be disadvantageous.

## Conservation

The plight of scaly reptiles with forked tongues does not stimulate a great response in most people. Having said this, the conservation of snakes often becomes a valuable by-product of large conservation programmes aimed primarily at species which have a more loveable public image, and although a few species enjoy protection in their own right, the future existence of snakes as a whole must be dependent upon the preservation of their habitats, whether these be rain forests, deserts, rivers and lakes or

Plate 69   The indigo snake, *Drymarchon corais couperi*, of south-eastern North America was afforded legal protection several years ago due to pressures of habitat destruction and over-collecting.

ocean reefs. Since we understand so little about them and their effect on the environment, it is important that they are conserved *in situ*, not as small breeding populations in zoos or carefully managed snake parks (although these may have their place where habitats are already doomed, such as with the Round Island boas). The fact is that, in many parts of the world, the snake fauna has not been fully investigated and we are undoubtedly exterminating some species before we even know of their existence – the priority must therefore be to stop, or even to reverse, the wholesale destruction of wild places.

Legal protection of individual species of snakes does occur (Plate 69), for instance in Britain, where the smooth snake, *Coronella austriaca*, is totally protected, and in the United States, where several species may not be collected or otherwise interfered with. More commonly, however, snakes enjoy blanket protection along with all other fauna – the collection and exportation of all wild animals is illegal in Papua New Guinea,

Australia, Brazil, many European and some Asian, countries. On the other hand, snakes may be systematically eliminated, as on the Greek island of Milos, where a bounty was placed on the viper, *Viper lebetina*, for many years, a particularly unfortunate state of affairs since Milos is the only European site for this otherwise Middle Eastern species – furthermore, the race found there, *V. l. schweitzeri*, is endemic to the island. In terms of numbers of animals killed, however, the most inexcusable extermination policy is found in parts of the United States, where 'rattlesnake roundups' impose a devastating toll on rattlesnakes (and also on other species sharing their habitats). These events consist of the capture of as many rattlesnakes as possible over a short period of time, usually with some element of competition between the participants. The means used to achieve this include digging out hibernacula where snakes often congregate in large numbers, and introducing petrol or motor-car exhaust fumes into burrows suspected of harbouring rattlesnakes. The captured snakes are brought together at the end of the period and after suffering various indignities are sold to snake sideshows, dealers, or killed (possibly to end up as canned rattlesnake).

# Chapter 9
# Snake Families

## Leptotyphlopidae – Thread Snakes

About 50 species in two genera make up this family, which is usually accepted as the most primitive of snakes. Their distribution (Map 2) covers most of tropical America and Africa, and extends into western Asia. They have a pelvic girdle and vestigial hind limbs, teeth are absent from the upper jaw and they have a single lung and oviduct. All are quite similar in appearance, being small (up to a maximum of 40 cm, 16 in) and slender, and they may be black, brown, or lacking in pigment altogether. A few have an indistinct pattern consisting of longitudinal stripes. They are all firmly tied to a burrowing life-style, having a blunt snout and short blunt tail, and they feed exclusively on small soft-bodied invertebrates such as ant, termite and other insect larvae, and some species are strongly associated with termite and ant nests, having been found only in these situations. Their mouths are small, as are their eyes, and their scales overlap each other and are highly polished.

Map 2  Distribution of the Leptotyphlopidae.

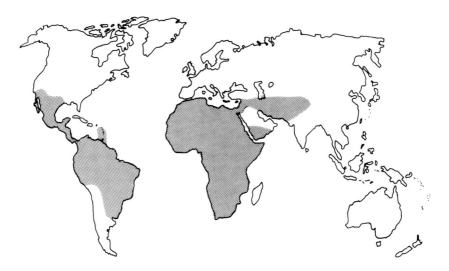

Plate 70   A thread snake, *Leptotyphlops humilis*, from North America. Note its small eyes, shiny scales and lack of pigment.

Specimens are most commonly found beneath logs or stones, when they are ploughed up, or when washed from their burrows by heavy rain or flooding. Little is known of their behaviour, but all of the species so far investigated appear to lay eggs: females of at least one species, *Leptotyphlops dulcis*, the Texas thread snake, coil around their clutches in underground chambers throughout incubation. Another American species, *L. humilis* (Plate 70) lays from 2 to 6 eggs from which relatively large young hatch, whereas the eggs of an African species, *L. conjuncta*, have been compared to grains of rice, both in shape and size!

## Typhlopidae – Blind Snakes

The blind snakes are all small, cylindrical snakes with glossy scales and a tail which ends in a blunt spine. Their eyes are covered by scales, and they have a vestigial pelvic girdle. There is a single oviduct (the right) and a single lung (also the right). They differ from other worm snakes (Lepto-

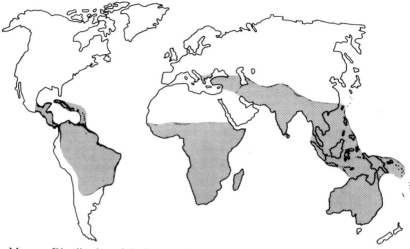

Map 3   Distribution of the Typhlopidae.

typhlopidae and Anomalepidae) in having teeth on the upper jaw only. Most are brown in colour, but some have faint reticulations on the head and longitudinal markings along their bodies.

The two genera occur over most of the warmer parts of the world (Map 3), typically living beneath the surface or in rotting logs etc, where they

Plate 71   The Brahminy worm snake, *Rhamphotyphlops braminus*, the only snake known to reproduce parthenogenetically (see page 64).

feed largely on termites and ants and their larvae. Some species prefer moist forest habitats, whilst others are found in sandy, arid regions. The genus *Typhlops* occurs in both the New and the Old Worlds, but the other genus, *Rhamphotyphlops* (formerly known as *Typhlina*) is restricted to the Old, especially Australia where 22 species are found. In the West Indies, about 16 species of *Typhlops* are recognised, each restricted to a single island or group of islands, an example of how a group of animals diversifies when their range is fragmented.

Most species appear to be oviparous, some laying 50 eggs or more (e.g. the African *Typhlops schegelii*), although 5–12 seems to be more usual. A few species, e.g. *T. diardii*, may retain their eggs until the point of hatching, or they may hatch just a few days after they are laid, but the reproductive biology of many species is completely unknown (many species are only known from one or two specimens). *Rhamphotyphlops braminus* (Plate 71) holds the distinction of being the only known parthenogenic snake – this, and its associated distributional peculiarities, are described in Chapter 4.

## Anomalepidae

The Anomalepidae is a small family consisting of about twenty species in four genera: *Liotyphlops*, *Anomalepis*, *Helminthophis* and *Typhlophis*. All are tiny thread-like snakes from tropical South America (Map 4), and they

Map 4    Distribution of the Anomalepidae.

differ from the worm snakes and thread snakes (Typhlopidae and Leptotyphlopidae) by lacking a vestigial pelvic girdle and by having teeth on both upper and lower jaws.

*Typhlophis squamosus* is reported to lay 2–6 eggs, and all the species live exclusively in underground burrows, but otherwise nothing appears to be known of their natural history.

## Uropeltidae – Shield-tailed Snakes

The Uropeltidae is a well-defined family of about 40 small burrowing snakes restricted to southern India and Sri Lanka (Map 5), where they live amongst roots beneath the forest floor (or in areas previously forested), mostly in hilly or mountainous regions. They rarely venture above the surface, and only do so when the soil has been soaked by rain. The largest species, *Pseudotyphlops philippinus*, grows to about 75 cm (30 in) in total length and 3 cm ($1\frac{1}{4}$ in) in diameter, but most are much smaller than this.

Uropeltids are characterised by several adaptations associated with their burrowing activities: the head is narrow and pointed and the neck very flexible; the eyes are reduced; ventral scales are small; and all scales are highly polished. As in other burrowing snakes, the tail is short, but that of the uropeltids is unique in terminating in a single, large, modified scale which is rough, and which may possess at least one, and often several, spines. In certain species, genus *Uropeltis*, the tail is obliquely truncated, the terminal shield therefore being oval in shape (Fig. 15). The purpose of these roughened scales is not definitely known, but may serve to plug the burrow of the snake as it progresses. The spines invariably

Map 5   Distribution of the Uropeltidae.

Fig. 15   The tails of snakes in the genus *Uropeltis* end in a large plate bearing numerous rugosities and spines.

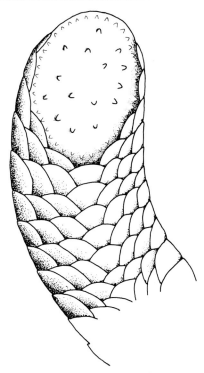

become clogged with soil particles and this may further confuse predators who may be chasing them. Earlier suggestions that the spines were used to gain purchase on the burrow wall and so help the snake to thrust its way through the soil appear to have been ill-founded. In fact, only the front one-third of the body is used in burrowing: the snake forms a series of curves in this region of its body and jams itself against both sides of the tunnel wall, enabling the head to be forced through the substrate. The body is then drawn up and the process repeated. Strangely, the curves of the body are not followed by the skin but only involve the muscles, backbone and ribs. The fore-part of the body thickens to accommodate this flexing.

Most uropeltids are dark in colour, although where they occur in light coloured soils they may be coloured accordingly. Many species have small areas of bright colouration, presumed to act as flash colours to startle predators (see page 55), although they may also serve to provide a superficial resemblance to poisonous snakes (kraits) or centipedes which occur in the same region. All species have highly iridescent scales as a result of their glossy surface, a condition which reduces friction and which is found in most other burrowing snakes; for instance, the sunbeam snake, Plate 72.

## Aniliidae – Pipe Snakes

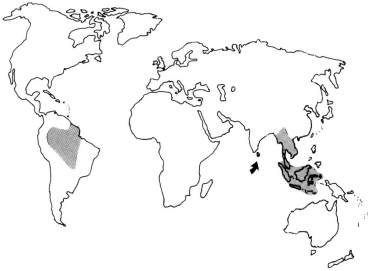

The pipe snakes are a small group of burrowing snakes consisting of nine species from India (genera *Cylindrophis* and *Anomochilus*) and a single species, *Anilius scytale*, from northern South America (Map 6). This disjunct distribution is difficult to explain and it may well be that further investigation will demand that the family be divided into two. However, all have vestigial hind limbs as well as similarities in the structure of their skulls. They also have enlarged ventral plates, a feature not seen in the preceding four families.

*Anilius scytale* is a beautiful red and black banded snake growing to about a metre (3 ft) in length. In Venezuela its resemblance to several of the venomous coral snakes, *Micrurus*, has earned it the common name of 'coral falsa'. It has a blunt snout and small eyes covered by a large transparent scale, differing in this respect from the Asian species which have a brille covering their eyes. It feeds on invertebrates, caecilians (burrowing legless amphibians), amphisbaenids and small lizards and snakes, bulkier prey being excluded owing to the limited amount of flexibility in the skull. It is ovo-viviparous, bearing 4–10 young.

The Asian pipe snakes, the best-known of which are the *Cylindrophis* species, are generally duller in colouration, being brown with few if any markings on their dorsal surface. Some species are boldly marked with red, orange, pink or white below, especially beneath their tails, which may be raised if the snake is threatened, thus exposing the bright aposematic colouration (see page 55). All are ovo-viviparous as far as is known.

*Cylindrophis rufus*, at 1 metre (3 ft) the largest species, is found in Indo-China where it inhabits marshy lowlands, including paddy-fields. It spends most of its time beneath the surface of the mud but also swims well, and feeds on eels as well as other snakes, often taking meals which exceed its own length.

## Xenopeltidae – Sunbeam Snake

The Xenopeltidae is the smallest family of snakes – it contains but a solitary species, *Xenopeltis unicolor*, the sunbeam snake (Plate 72), which is distinct in having the following combination of features: both lungs present, as in some boids, but no vestigial hind limbs or pelvis. It also has a rigid skull (primitive), but large ventral scales and a brille covering the eye (advanced).

*Xenopeltis* is a burrowing snake which only appears on the surface during the night. In keeping with these habits it is cylindrical in cross-section, and its scales are smooth, shiny and highly iridescent. It is dark brown dorsally, white ventrally and grows to about 1.3 m ($4\frac{1}{4}$ ft) in length.

Its distribution (Map 7) takes in much of South-east Asia from Burma

Plate 72    The sunbeam snake, *Xenopeltis unicolor*, from South-east Asia, the only member of its family.

Map 7    Distribution of the Xenopeltidae.

to southern China, and it is said to be very common in places, for instance in Thailand. In spite of this, its habits are not well-known: its diet apparently consists of rodents, other snakes and amphibians but, amazingly, nothing whatsoever appears to be known of its breeding habits.

## Boidae – Boas and Pythons

This family contains all five of the 'giant snakes' as well as a number of small to medium-sized species. It is an ancient family with many extinct

**Table 5:    Sub-families of Boidae (the Boas and Pythons)**

| Sub-family | Distribution | Approx. no. of species | Typical genus | Reproduction |
|---|---|---|---|---|
| Boinae | Americas, Malagasy, Papua New Guinea | 26 | *Boa* *Sanzinia* *Candoia* | Ovo-viviparous |
| Bolyerinae | Round Island | 2 | *Bolyeria* | Apparently unknown |
| Calabarinae | Africa | 1 | *Calabaria* | Oviparous |
| Erycinae | Africa, Asia | 25 | *Eryx* | Ovo-viviparous |
| Loxoceminae | Central America | 1 | *Loxocemus* | Apparently unknown |
| Pythoninae | Africa, Asia, Australasia | 20 | *Python* *Liasis* | Oviparous: clutch-brooding in some spe |
| Tropidophinae | Central America | 20+ | *Tropidophis* | Ovo-viviparous |

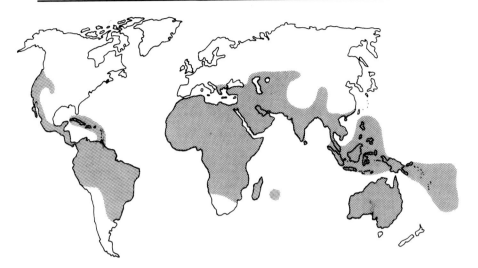

Map 8    Distribution of the Boidae.

forms, and the surviving species are found in a wide range of habitats and
their appearance is therefore equally diverse. Anatomically, their most
important characteristics are the flexible jaws, not found in the previous
six (more primitive) families and the presence of vestigial hind limbs and
a pelvic girdle, not found in the following four (more advanced) families.
In addition, the left lung as well as the right may be functional, a primitive
condition found in only one other snake (*Xenopeltis unicolor*).

There is some controversy over the relationships of the various members of this family, but the generally accepted arrangement is to recognise
seven sub-families: Boinae (boas); Bolyerinae (Round Island boas);
Calabarinae (Calabar ground python); Erycinae (sand boas, rubber boa
and rosy boa); Loxoceminae (Mexican dwarf boa); Pythoninae (pythons);
and Tropidophinae (dwarf boas). See Map 8.

## Boinae – Boas

The Boinae is a very widespread sub-family if the present grouping is
accepted. About 20 species occur in Central and South America, three in
Madagascar and three in Papua New Guinea and neighbouring islands.
All give birth to living young, and those species which have facial pits
(genera *Epicrates*, *Corallus* and *Sanzinia*) have them between the scales
bordering the upper lip. All are powerful constrictors. Largest of the
sub-family is undoubtedly *Eunectes murinus*, the legendary anaconda, which

Plate 73 (opposite above)   The rainbow boa, *Epicrates cenchria*, a widespread South American species.

Plate 74 (opposite below)   Cook's tree boa, *Corallus enhydris*, from South America. Note its facial pits.

Plate 75   The Pacific ground boa, *Candoia aspera*, is a common species from Papua New Guinea and neighbouring islands, where it inhabits the forest floor.

may grow to 10 m (33 ft) or more in length. This gigantic snake is found throughout the northern part of South America and, although it is usually associated with water, it also climbs well.

Its food consists mainly of mammals, but turtles and caimans are also eaten. In colour it is dull yellow, with bold black markings along its length, its scales being smooth and glossy. It is notorious for its irascibility, a characteristic shared by its close, but much smaller, relative, the yellow anaconda, *E. notaeus*.

The common boa, *Boa constrictor* (Plate 16), at about half the maximum size of the anaconda, suffers from acute exaggeration at the hands of travellers and showmen. In fact, it is 'only' the fifth or sixth largest snake in the world. This is an extremely adaptable species, occurring in semi-desert regions (in Mexico) as well as in its more familiar habitat of moist rain forests, where it normally lives amongst the tree-tops, coming down to the ground only to forage. It is commonly found around human habitations, attracted there by the possibility of good hunting for rats and mice (and the occasional chicken or other domestic animal). Its markings are variable and a number of subspecies have been described, but typically it is a grey or silver snake with a series of brown or deep red saddles along its back, these becoming more reddish towards the tail. Specimens from the south of the range (*B. c. occidentalis*, the Argentine boa) are dark in colour and have a network of silver reticulations over the entire body. The common boa gives birth to 30–50 young, each about 30 cm (1 ft) in total length.

The genus *Epicrates* contains several species from South America and the Caribbean region. The commonest, *E. cenchria* (Plate 73), is known as the rainbow boa owing to the iridescence of its scales. A number of subspecies are recognised, the most wide-ranging being the nominate one, *E. c. cenchria*. This snake is orange to mahogany in colour with a row of dark circles along its dorsal midline, but these markings are not easily distinguished in old animals of the darker races. Unlike the previous two genera, *Epicrates* species have heat-sensitive pits, probably due to their almost exclusively nocturnal habits. During the day they usually rest in trees or amongst the rafters of old buildings.

*Corallus* is a small South American genus of nocturnal and arboreal species with facial pits. *C. enhydris* (Plate 74) is quite small, growing to a maximum length of about 1.5 m (5 ft). In feeding, it appears to have a preference for birds but, like most boas, it will also take mammals. *Corallus caninus*, the emerald tree boa (Plate 23), has a more restricted range than *C. enhydris* and is especially remarkable for its resemblance to *Chondropython viridis*, an Australasian species (Plate 22). In colour it is bright green above with irregular white markings along its dorsal midline, the underside being pale to bright yellow. This is a strongly arboreal species, rarely coming down to the ground, but habitually draping its coils over a horizontal branch. Like *C. enhydris*, it feeds on birds, bats and arboreal mammals, its prehensile tail providing a secure anchor as it strikes, constricts and swallows its prey whilst hanging head down from a bough.

Leaving the New World, the three species of Boidae inhabiting Madagascar consist of an arboreal species with a prehensile tail, *Sanzinia madagascariensis*, and two ground-dwelling species, *Acrantophis madagascariensis* and *A. dumerillii*. *Sanzinia* is variable in colouration, ususally yellowish or greenish with dark transverse markings. It possesses facial pits and probably feeds largely upon roosting birds and bats. The two species of *Acrantophis* bear a superficial resemblance to the common boa in appearance but both are terrestrial.

In Papua New Guinea and neighbouring islands, three small boids belonging to the genus *Candoia* represent this sub-family. All are found in forest habitats, and all are remarkably well camouflaged. *Candoia aspera* (Plate 75) is a typical terrestrial species – heavy-bodied and slow-moving – measuring just over 0.5 m ($1\frac{1}{2}$ ft) maximum. *C. bibroni*, by contrast, is an arboreal species and is more slender, growing to just over 1 m (3 ft), whereas the remaining species, *C. carinata*, is intermediate in habits, size and form – a neat example of resource partitioning amongst three closely related species living in close proximity (see Chapter 7). All three are characterised by their sharply angled snouts and, due to their markings, are sometimes known as 'viper boas'. All appear to eat small rodents and lizards, lying in wait to ambush their prey and then striking rapidly and constricting it in their very powerful coils.

## Bolyerinae – Round Island Boas

The sub-family Bolyerinae consists of only two species, *Bolyeria multicarinata*, and *Casarea dusumieri*, both of which live on Round Island in the Indian Ocean. They are unique amongst the Boidae in lacking vestigial hind limbs or a pelvic girdle. Due to erosion and human interference on this island, these species are in serious danger of becoming extinct, along with the rest of the island's fauna. Since these small boas appear to be a link in the evolutionary chain between the Boidae and the Colubridae, this would be particularly disastrous. Both are small, ground-dwelling species which probably feed largely on lizards, otherwise almost nothing is known of their natural history.

## Calabarinae – Calabar Ground Python

Sub-family Calabarinae has only one species, *Calabaria reinhardtii*, the Calabar ground python. This medium-sized snake (up to about 1 m, 3 ft) is mainly fossorial, burrowing into rodent galleries in search of food. In colour it may be red, orange, yellow or white with black bands and blotches. The head and tail are both black and blunt, and when threatened this species often forms a ball with the head protected amongst

Plate 76  *Loxocemus bicolor* is a little-known and enigmatic boa from Mexico. In many ways it resembles the sunbeam snake, Plate 72.

its coils and the tail exposed. A recent report suggests that it lays a small number of eggs.

## Erycinae – Sand Boas, Rubber Boa and Rosy Boa

Sub-family Erycinae occurs in both the New and Old Worlds. The two North American species are *Lichanura trivirgata*, the rosy boa, ranging from California down into Mexico, and *Charina bottae*, the rubber boa, which has a slightly more northerly range in Western North America. *Lichanura* may be found in dry desert areas as well as along the cooler coastal belt, but *Charina* is restricted to higher altitudes and is typically found amongst pine forests, e.g. in the Sierra Nevada. It is largely crepuscular and, like the Calabar ground python and the sand boas (see below) may raise its blunt tail when threatened as a means of mimetic defence.

In the Old World, a number of species belonging to the genus *Eryx* represent this sub-family. These 'sand boas' typically inhabit dry areas in Africa, western Asia and south-eastern Europe. Like the two American species, they rarely exceed 1 m (3 ft) in length and, being burrowing

Plate 77   The reticulated python, one of the world's giants, which may exceed 9 m (30 ft) in length.

snakes, they all have thick-set cylindrical bodies with a blunt or shovel-shaped snout and a blunt tail. In some species the eyes point upwards so that they are able to see whilst partially buried in sand or loose earth, and they feed on small mammals and lizards. Most of them are cryptically-coloured to blend in with the substrate in which they live, although they rarely move about on the surface during the day. All species in this sub-family give birth to living young, and none of them have facial pits. *Eryx jaculus*, the javelin sand boa, shown in its defensive posture in Plate 54, ranges over much of western Asia and into the extreme south-eastern part of Europe where it is the only representative of the Boidae. It can be found beneath rocks on dry barren hillsides and in fields, where ·it is sometimes brought to light by the plough.

## Loxoceminae – Mexican Dwarf Boa

Sub-family Loxoceminae has only one member, *Loxocemus bicolor*, the Mexican dwarf boa (Plate 76). This snake has created many problems for taxonomists and it may be found classified alongside the pipe snakes (Aniliidae) or even placed in a family of its own (Loxocemidae). Most

Plate 78   The Indian python, *Python molurus*, a species which 'broods' its eggs.

authorities, however, recognise it as a primitive boa. It also bears strong superficial and anatomical resemblances to another odd-ball, with a similar name, *Xenopeltis unicolor*, the sunbeam snake or iridescent earth snake. *Loxocemus* occurs in the west of Mexico, where it probably spends most of its time below ground. Few specimens are collected and very little is known about its behaviour and ecology.

## Pythoninae – Pythons

Members of the sub-family Pythoninae, however, are much more familiar, including as they do three of the world's largest snakes – *Python reticulatus*, *P. sebae* and *P. molurus*. All pythons have heat-sensitive pits located in their upper lips but, whereas in boas these are placed between the scales, in the pythons they are *within* each scale (Plates 22 and 23). Pythons also differ from boas by laying eggs, and there is strong evidence to suggest that some species are able to raise the temperature within each clutch by coiling around it (see also Chapter 4). Pythons probably hunt by day and night, feeding mainly upon mammals and birds, which their facial pits are best able to detect.

The largest species, *P. reticulatus*, the reticulated python (Plate 77), reaches a length approaching 10 m (33 ft) and vies with the anaconda for the title of the world's largest snake, although it is more slender and lighter than its South American counterpart. Its home is in the forests of South-east Asia and Indonesia, where its intricate pattern camouflages it well in areas of light and shade. This species has been reported to lay over 100 eggs which the female guards by coiling around them, but, unlike the Indian python (see below), their temperature does not appear to be elevated above that of their surroundings.

Also in South-east Asia is another large python, *P. molurus* (Plate 78), which exists in two forms: *P. molurus molurus*, the 'light phase' or Indian python, and *P. molurus bivittatus*, the 'dark phase' or Burmese python. The latter is the commonest and largest, growing to a maximum of about 6.5 m (21 ft), and becomes quite docile in captivity, making it the most popular species with exotic dancers! This species has been bred many times in captivity, clutches of between 25 and 60 eggs having been reported. Throughout their incubation, which takes about 100 days, these are guarded by the female, who coils around them and leaves only occasionally to drink. The temperature of the eggs may be raised several degrees above that of their surroundings by means of a process which is not yet fully understood but which appears to be associated with twitching movements made by the female during the brooding period. Interestingly, if the eggs are removed experimentally, the female will continue to twitch occasionally, despite the absence of her clutch.

A third member of the genus *Python* from this region is *P. curtus*, known as the blood python because some specimens are suffused with orange or

Plate 79   D'Albertis' python, *Liasis albertisi*, belongs to a genus which is restricted to Australasia.

red. This stocky species hails from the humid regions of Indonesia and adjacent South-east Asia.

In Africa the largest species is *Python sebae*, the African rock python, growing almost as long as the reticulated python – to 9.8 m (32 ft). This species has a wide range over central and southern Africa, occurring right down to the temperate regions of the Cape. It is at home in a variety of habitats but favours fairly open bush or scrub and has a predilection for rocky outcrops. This species frequently includes small antelopes, wild pigs and monkeys in its diet, as well as smaller game. About 50, but occasionally up to 100, eggs are laid and guarded by the female.

*Python anchietae*, the Angolan python, has a much more restricted range in Angola and Namibia, and grows to only about 1.5 m (5 ft). It is one of the rarities amongst the pythons and consequently little is known about its habits, but a clutch size of five eggs has been reported. *P. regius*, the royal python, completes the African trio, and is a small thick-set snake with a short tail. Its habit of rolling up with its head in the centre of its coils has earned it the alternative name of 'ball python'. It too lays few eggs (up to eight), and these are coiled around by the female, who may raise their temperature slightly.

The Australasian region is particularly rich in pythons, including several interesting species. These show great diversity of form and habitat and range in size from the amethystine python, *Liasis amethystinus* (to 4 m, 13 ft, but occasionally much longer), down to the recently described *Liasis perthensis*, a diminutive python which rarely exceeds 50 cm (20 in) in length and often lives in termite mounds where it feeds on a small gecko, *Gehyra pilbara*, also associated with the insects. (*L. perthensis* may actually be a subspecies of *L. childreni*, a slightly larger form with a wide range over Australia.) Three other species of *Liasis* occur in the region – *L. fuscus*, a medium-sized species associated with water, *L. olivaceous*, the olive python, and *L. oenpelliensis*, a recently discovered species vying with the amethystine species in size. In Papua New Guinea, a seventh species, *L. albertisi* (Plate 79), is found.

The single species belonging to the genus *Chondrophython, C. viridis*, has been mentioned elsewhere in connection with its adaptation to an arboreal life-style and its similarity to a boa, *Corallus caninus*. This species is quite common on the island of Papua New Guinea, and just reaches the Australian mainland on the extreme northern tip of Queensland, where it lives in tropical rain forests. It may reach 2 m ($6\frac{1}{2}$ ft) but is usually about half this in length and lays between 10 and 20 eggs. The young, on hatching, may be bright yellow or brick red, a colouration which persists for about two years before the transition to the bright green of the adult takes place. This is the only example of a distinct juvenile form amongst pythons.

*Morelia spilotes* is another common Australian and Papuan species which has adapted to a variety of habitats from rain forests to deserts. It climbs well but may also live below ground in animal burrows and is commonly found in the vicinity of human settlements. At least two forms are recognised, *M. spilotes spilotes*, the diamond python, a dark subspecies speckled with white, cream or yellow, and the carpet python, *M. spilotes variegata*, which is brown or grey with yellow blotches and bars. A variety of other types occur, some of which may be regarded as separate subspecies, but expert opinion is by no means unanimous. Carpet and diamond pythons lay about 10 to 40 eggs which they protect, and possibly brood.

The final genus of Australasian pythons, *Aspidites*, unlike those dealt with so far, is restricted to the Australian mainland. It is unusual in that its two members lack the facial heat-sensitive pits found in all other pythons. The two species are rather similar in size (to about 1.5 m, 5 ft, but occasionally larger) and general appearance. Both are basically brown, but *A. melanocephalus*, the black-headed python, has a distinctive black head which is lacking in *A. ramsayi*, known as the woma. Both species eat reptiles, including venomous snakes, as well as amphibians, birds and small mammals, and both lay clutches of less than 10 eggs.

## Tropidophinae – Dwarf Boas

The dwarf boas of the Caribbean region (Tropidophinae) complete the family. Most are placed in the genus *Tropidophis*, 12 species of which are scattered throughout the West Indian Islands with another three on the mainland. Three other genera, *Trachyboa*, *Exiliboa* and *Ungaliophis*, are confined to Central America and northern South America. These small and secretive snakes are all terrestrial (except one species) and are found beneath logs etc. They appear to feed mainly upon lizards, but probably take small mammals and frogs occasionally. In keeping with their habitat, all are brown in colour, a form of protection which is supplemented dramatically in *Tropidophis* species, which produce an evil-smelling fluid from their cloaca and squeeze blood from their eyes if they are molested.

## Acrochordidae – Wart Snakes

This family consists of only three species (until recently only two were recognised), all in the genus *Acrochordus*. Although they share many features with advanced snakes such as the Colubridae (single lung, absence of hind-limbs or pelvic girdle and a flexible skull), their most notable characteristics are those associated with a totally aquatic way of life, for these species inhabit rivers, estuaries and coastal waters in South-east Asia, Indonesia, Papua New Guinea and northern Australia (Map 9). Their skin is loose and hangs in folds around their bodies, and is covered with numerous granular scales (Plate 11), making it popular in the hide industry, where it is known as karung. They have no ventral

Map 9  Distribution of the Acrochordidae.

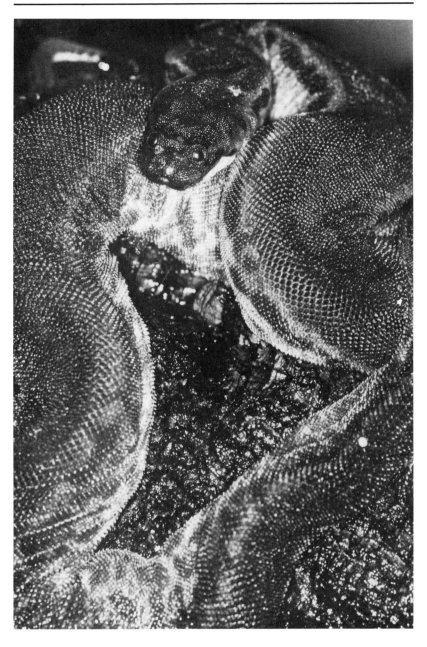

Plate 80  *Acrochordus javanicus*, one of three species of wart snakes, and sometimes known as the elephant's trunk snake.

plates, although one species, *A. granulatus*, has a ridge-like structure running along its ventral midline which aids in swimming. The nostrils may be closed by means of a flap on the roof of the mouth, and the notch where the tongue is protruded (lingual fossa) can also be sealed by a flap on their chin. Salt glands are present at the base of the sheath housing the tongue.

The natural history of wart snakes is not well-known as they are difficult to study in the wild, and do not easily adapt to captivity, but all are ovo-viviparous, a necessity for species which are practically helpless on land. Nothing is known of their gestation period. All three are sluggish in their movements and are largely nocturnal, and all appear to prey entirely on fish, with a few reports of marine invertebrates having been eaten.

Although there are areas of overlap in the ranges of the three species, they are separated largely by habitat preference. *Acrochordus javanicus* (Plate 80) is predominantly a freshwater species ranging from Thailand, through Malaya and as far as the Greater Sunda Islands. *A. granulatus* (formerly known as *Chersydrus granulatus*) is found in estuaries and coastal waters around India, the Malay peninsula, Papua New Guinea and northern Australia. It differs from the other species in having a laterally compressed tail. *A. arafurae*, a recently described species, is the largest wart snake, attaining over 1.5 m (5 ft) in total length. Like *A. javanicus*, it is a freshwater form but it is found only in rivers entering the south coast of Papua New Guinea and the north coast of Australia.

## Colubridae – Typical Snakes

The family Colubridae, most usually referred to as 'typical' snakes for want of a better name, consists of over 2,000 species, making it far larger than all the other families put together. Moreover, it is the dominant family in all geographical regions except Australia, where the cobra family (Elapidae) predominates. Most colubrids are medium-sized snakes with enlarged ventral scales and a brille covering the eye. They do not possess a vestigial pelvic girdle or limbs and the left lung is reduced or absent altogether. Owing to their huge range (Map 10) and the diversity of habitats occupied by these snakes, many variations exist within this theme, and it is convenient to deal with the species, as with the Boidae, by sub-family. Eight of these are recognised by many authorities, but the division of such a large and varied group of animals is bound to create differences of opinion and the constant revision of groupings is something of a problem.

The majority of species are placed in two large sub-families, the Colubrinae and the Natricinae, distinguished only by a minor skeletal difference: the Natricinae have spines on the lumbar vertebrae, whereas the Colubrinae do not. About 290 genera are recognised within the

146

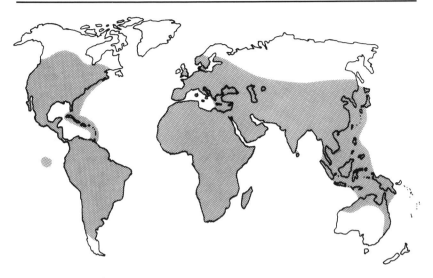

Map 10    Distribution of the Colubridae.

Colubrinae: an enormous number of animals to be lumped together in this way, and further divisions seem inevitable. It is only possible here to mention some of the more common and more interesting kinds.

## Colubrinae

It seems appropriate to start an account of this sub-family with snakes of the genus *Coluber*, since this has not only given the sub-family and family its name, but stems from the classical name for all snakes (derivatives of which are still to be found in many Latin languages: *culebra* – Spanish; *couleuvre* – French). The genus *Coluber* is one of the few which are found in both the New and Old Worlds. In Europe they are known as whipsnakes and include such species as *C. viridiflavus*, a common species in central Europe, *C. gemonensis* (Plate 81) from the Balkan peninsula, and *C. hippocrepis* (Plate 4) from southern Spain and Portugal. All of these and several others are typical diurnal snakes – they have long slender bodies and move rapidly through the light vegetation or scrub which covers much of the region in which they live. Their pupils are round and their vision is good, an essential quality for species which hunt their prey (mainly lizards) actively. In North America the genus is represented by only one species, *Coluber constrictor*, the racer, which has a wide range and several subspecies. In habits it conforms to the same general pattern as the European species.

A second genus which is found on both sides of the Atlantic is *Elaphe*,

147

Plate 81  A typical colubrine, the Balkan whipsnake, *Coluber gemonensis*.

Plate 82  Juvenile *Elaphe scalaris* have a dorsal pattern which provides their common name of ladder snake. They are found in Spain.

members of which are known collectively as ratsnakes. Five or six species come from North America, the most common of which is *Elaphe obsoleta*. This variable species occurs in several distinct geographical forms, all differing in colour or markings, for instance the Texas, black or grey ratsnake etc. In common with some other *Elaphe* species, *E. obsoleta* undergoes a change in appearance as it grows: at hatching the juveniles are pale grey with a series of dark blotches or saddles along their back; as they mature these markings become less distinct and may be replaced by a uniform colouration (as in the black ratsnake, *E. o. obsoleta*) or by four longitudinal lines (e.g. the yellow ratsnake, *E. o. quadrivittata*). Only one subspecies, the grey ratsnake, *E. o. spiloides*, retains the juvenile pattern throughout its life.

*Elaphe guttata*, the corn snake or red ratsnake (Plate 41), is a popular species with zoos and private collectors due to its attractive colouration, and *E. subocularis*, the trans-pecos ratsnake, is unusual amongst the genus in being entirely nocturnal. European species include the ladder snake, *E. scalaris* (Plate 82), the four-lined snake, *E. quatuorlineata*, a large species which goes through a similar pattern change to the yellow ratsnake (Plates 33 and 34), and *E. situla*, the leopard snake (Plate 28), a small but attractive species from eastern Europe. All of these, and other members of the genus from North America, Europe and Asia, lay eggs. Most are opportunities feeders, taking mainly small rodents but also the odd lizard, frog or invertebrate, and all are powerful constrictors, capable of taking relatively large prey. Several are good climbers but, in general, ratsnakes are terrestrial species.

The genus *Lampropeltis* (kingsnakes and milk snakes) contains several of the most colourful colubrids. These are the false coral snakes, such as *L. pyromelana woodini* (Plate 30) from Arizona and *L. zonata* (Plate 83) from California. These tri-coloured snakes are marked with red, black and white rings in the same manner as several of the venomous coral snakes and have long been considered mimics of them (but see page 53). Other kingsnakes are marked with black and white (Plates 31 and 32) or with brown and red saddles. All eat rodents, birds, reptiles and amphibians, depending on availability, and some species are looked upon favourably by the general public as they feed on venomous snakes, especially rattlesnakes. They occur over a wide area and inhabit the northern forests of Canada, through a wide variety of temperate habitats to the deserts and mountains of California, Arizona and Mexico and the tropical rain forests of South America. Indeed, the most northerly species, *L. triangulum*, is also the most southerly, although populations from these two extremes are dissimilar in appearance and are distinct subspecies separated geographically by a number of intermediate forms.

Plate 83 (overleaf)   The Californian mountain kingsnake, *Lampropeltis zonata*, a boldly marked 'false coral' snake.

*Drymarchon corais*, known as the indigo snake or cribo, is the largest colubrid in the Americas, where it is found from Florida to Brazil. This species may reach almost 3 m (10 ft) in length and is a handsome, fast-moving snake which includes other snakes, mammals, amphibians and fish in its diet. The largest colubrid of all, however, is the Asian ratsnake, *Ptyas mucosus*, which grows to 3.5 m ($11\frac{1}{2}$ ft). Due to its size and abundance (at least at the moment), this species is heavily exploited for its skin.

## Natricinae – Semi-aquatic Snakes

Closely related to the Colubrinae, and almost equal to it in size, is the sub-family Natricinae. Many of the species in this sub-family are associated with a semi-aquatic environment and include the North American genera *Nerodia* (water snakes) (Plate 84) and *Thamnophis* (garter and ribbon snakes). These snakes have heavily keeled scales, feed primarily on fish and amphibians (and, in some cases, earthworms), and give birth to living young (occasionally 100 or more at a time). In suitable habitats, these snakes may be extremely abundant, and hibernacula containing several hundred individuals have been discovered. On the other hand, in areas where water is scarce, populations may be very small, for instance, the San Francisco garter snake, *Thamnophis sirtalis tetrataenia*, is all but extinct owing to the development of its very limited range.

Plate 84 *Nerodia taxispilota* is one of several species of North American semi-aquatic natricine snakes.

Plate 85 *Natrix tessellata* is one of four European snakes which are closely related to *Nerodia* species but differ in that they lay eggs.

In Europe and Asia, snakes of the genus *Natrix* are the counterparts of these species but differ in being oviparous. Some species, e.g. *N. tessellata* (Plate 85), are aquatic in habit, but others, such as *N. natrix*, the grass snake, are not as closely associated with water and may occur in fairly dry regions, although all swim well and depend mainly upon fish and amphibians for their food.

## Back-fanged Colubrids

All members of the Colubrinae and Natricinae mentioned so far are non-venomous. However, a proportion of the species in these sub-families do produce venom and several have specialised grooved fangs towards the rear of their mouths which help it to find its way into the prey as it is being chewed. Only the larger species amongst these back-fanged, or opisthoglyphic, snakes are dangerous to man, the smaller ones being incapable of bringing the venom fangs into play on anything larger than the prey on which they feed.

The most notorious of these back-fanged species are the boomslang, *Dispholidus typus*, and the twig snake, *Thelotornis kirtlandi*, both arboreal African species, and both have caused the death of human beings,

Plate 86    The mangrove snake, *Boiga dendrophila*, is a large Asian back-fanged species which is probably not dangerous to man.

Plate 87    A young Montepellier snake, *Malpolon monspessulanus*, from southern Europe and North Africa. This large back-fanged species is diurnal and favours dry scrub and rocky habitats.

Plate 88   The cat snake, *Telescopus fallax*, a small back-fanged species which hunts sleeping lizards at night.

including at least two eminent herpetologists. Other species which may be dangerous to man are the Asian keelback, *Rhabdophis subminiatus*, and the larger members of the genera *Boiga* and *Psammophis*. The former is a large genus occurring in Africa, Asia and Australia, and includes the strikingly marked mangrove snake, *B. dendrophila* (Plate 86), whilst snakes of the genus *Psammophis* are confined to Africa and the Middle East where they are known as sand snakes. The largest and most widespread is *P. sibilans*, the hissing sand snake, a common and aggressive species which may reach over 1.5 m (5 ft). Whereas *Boiga* is a genus of mainly arboreal snakes, *Psammophis* species are more at home on the ground. One other large, and therefore potentially dangerous, species is the Montpellier snake, *Malpolon monspessulanus* (Plate 87), from southern Europe, North Africa and the Middle East. This species grows to 2 m ($6\frac{1}{2}$ ft) and is a fast diurnal hunter, preying on mammals, birds and reptiles. Staying in the Old World, other noteworthy, but probably harmless, opisthoglyphs are those belonging to the genera *Telescopus*, the tiger or cat snakes (Plate 88), *Chrysopelea*, the flying snakes, *Dryophis*, the tree snakes (Plate 48), and *Rhabdophis*, an Asian genus of natricine snakes which were thought for many years to be completely harmless until several unfortunate victims proved otherwise.

Plate 89    The Californian lyre snake, *Trimorphodon lambda*, a nocturnal desert species.

In the New World, few, if any, back-fanged species are dangerous to man but the group is well represented by a number of genera, including the lyre snakes, *Trimorphodon* (Plate 89); black-headed snakes, *Tantilla*; the mussurana, *Clelia clelia*, which feeds mainly on other snakes, including pit vipers; and the vine snakes, *Oxybelis*, slender, long-nosed creatures which parallel *Dryophis* in appearance and behaviour.

## Homalopsinae – Water Snakes

It is convenient at this point to move on to a sub-family of colubrids which are *all* back-fanged – the Homalopsinae. The 35 or so species are all more or less aquatic and are adapted accordingly: their eyes and nostrils point upwards; their tails are compressed; and all are viviparous. One species, *Erpeton tentaculatum* (Plate 90), being totally aquatic, has even lost the wide ventral scales found in all other colubrids and is completely helpless on land. Members of this sub-family, which are all small and therefore considered harmless to man, are confined to South-east Asia, Papua New Guinea and northern Australia. The largest genus is *Enhydris*, with about 25 species, whereas nine other genera consist of only one or two species each. Most homalopsid snakes feed on fish and frogs, but *Fordonia* (two species) also eat crabs.

156

## Dasypeltinae – Egg-eating Snakes

The Dasypeltinae is a small group of African colubrids known as the egg-eating snakes. The six species in this sub-family, all in the genus *Dasypeltis* (although an Asian species, *Elachistodon westermanni*, which is an opisthoglyph, is sometimes placed in this sub-family), are justly famous for their ability to engulf birds' eggs of relatively huge proportions (see pages 79). The commonest species is *D. scabra*, a variable species which may imitate the venomous saw-scaled viper, *Echis carinata*, in appearance and threat behaviour in places where their ranges overlap. All dasypeltids are small in size, the largest species (*D. scaber*) averaging about 60 cm (2 ft), and all are oviparous, *D. scaber* laying 6–18 eggs.

## Dipsadinae – Mollusc-eating Snakes

The Dipsadinae are confined to South America, where the 60 or so species, belonging to three genera (*Dipsas, Sibon* and *Sibonomorphus*) specialise in eating land molluscs. To enable them to extract snails from their shells, they have an unusual arrangement whereby the lower jaw can be thrust forward into the snail's shell (see page 77). All of these species are slender arboreal snakes with a characteristically wide head and blunt snout (Plate 91), and all are nocturnal, their large eyes having vertically slit pupils. They live in the dense rain forests which cover most of their range, resting during the day amongst branches and epiphytic plants, where they are almost impossible to detect.

## Pareinae – Slug-eating Snakes

In Asia, another small sub-family, the Pareinae, parallel the Dipsinae closely and are known as slug-eating snakes. The 16 species are divided into two genera, *Pareas* and *Aplopeltura*. Because their jaws do not have to open widely to engulf the soft-bodied animals on which they prey, these snakes do not have the fold of skin (mental groove) beneath the chin which other snakes possess (of the previous sub-family, in only *Dipsas* is this also absent). Like dipsids, members of this sub-family are nocturnal and most are arboreal, although a few are terrestrial. *Pareas margaritophorus* is a typical example found throughout Indo-China. It averages about 30 cm (1 ft), is nocturnal and lives in moist forests.

## Xenodermatinae

The Xenodermatinae is possibly the most primitive sub-family of colubrids and its members show certain similarities to the wart snakes, Acrochordidae, including a tendency towards granular scales. This sub-family comprises four genera of secretive snakes from South-east Asia,

Plate 90    The fishing snake, *Erpeton tentaculatum*, belongs to the sub-family
Homolopsinae, the members of which are aquatic.

which are probably all nocturnal in habit. *Achalinus rufescens* is a small
species from Southern China and Japan, where it occurs at fairly high
altitudes. It apparently feeds on small invertebrates.

## Aparallactinae – Mole Vipers

The final, and most enigmatic, sub-family of colubrid snakes is the
Aparallactinae. The 17 genera placed in this group are all burrowing
snakes and all occur in Africa, with two species extending into the Middle
East. They are small cylindrical snakes with short blunt tails and small
eyes and all are venomous. They are unusual in having few, if any, teeth
other than elongated venom fangs on their upper jaw. Species of *Atractaspis*
are known as 'mole vipers' and were formerly classified with the true
vipers. These snakes have long hinged fangs that can be folded or erected
as desired in the same manner as those of the vipers, but they differ in that
the folded fangs can be exposed by moving the lower jaw out of the way,
and these species can therefore bite without opening their mouths. The

158

Plate 91    *Sibon nebulata*, a small arboreal member of the Dipsadinae, a neotropical
sub-family of mollusc-eating snakes.

advantages of such an arrangement are not clear, but it may enable them to catch their prey whilst in narrow burrows. Like other members of the Aparallactinae, they are probably not dangerous to man although bites from at least one species, *A. bibronii*, can cause swelling and pain, and may result in lingering symptoms such as stiff joints in the region of the bite. It feeds on other snakes, particularly fossorial species, lizards and the young of burrowing mammals, which it takes at night when it is most active. It grows to just over 60 cm (2 ft).

*Aparallactus* species, of which there are about 12, are known as centipede-eaters. The largest of these grows to about 50 cm (20 in) in length and, as may be expected, these snakes include centipedes amongst their prey, which they kill before eating by chewing along their bodies until the fast-acting venom takes effect. *A. capensis*, one of the most common species, grows to about 30 cm (1 ft) and is active at night, hiding beneath rocks and logs during the day.

Snakes of the genus *Xenocalamus* have long cylindrical heads and are known as quill-snouted snakes. They hunt other burrowing reptiles, especially amphisbaenians (worm 'lizards'), and are amongst the most brightly marked of the Aparallactinae, most of which are uniformly brown or black in colour.

To summarise a rather chaotic and unwieldy family, Table 6 lists the sub-families with some of their more important characteristics.

## Elapidae – Cobras and their allies

The cobra family is presumed to have evolved from the Colubridae, from which it differs in having a more efficient system for injecting venom: the fangs are effectively tubular (the venom-carrying grooves being enclosed by an infolding of their edges), and they are positioned at the front of the mouth where they may be brought into use more easily. Superficially, the most familiar of them resemble the colubrids, being moderately slender with large scales covering the head. However, there are a large number of secretive burrowing species; a few slender arboreal species; and two Australian species which, in body shape, parallel the vipers (a family which is absent from this region).

### Elapinae – Cobras, Coral Snakes, Mambas, Kraits

All of the terrestrial elapids are contained in a single sub-family, the Elapinae, containing about 120 species (Map 11). In the New World they are represented by a group of brightly-coloured nocturnal or crepuscular species, known collectively as coral snakes, genera *Micrurus* and *Micruroides*. These snakes, of which there are about 40 species covering the area between the southern United States to northern Argentina, are nearly all

**Table 6:  Sub-families of Colubridae**

| Sub-family | Distribution | Approx. no. of species | Fangs? | Typical genus | Remarks |
|---|---|---|---|---|---|
| Colubrinae | Cosmopolitan | 2,000 | Some species (back) | Coluber | Re-organisation inevitable. Oviparous, viviparous and ovo-viviparous species represented. |
| Natricinae | Cosmopolitan | | Some species (back) | Natrix | High degree of diversification. |
| Homalopsinae | Asia | 34 | Yes (back) | Homalopsis | Aquatic. Ovo-viviparous. |
| Dasypeltinae | Africa | 6 | No | Dasypeltis | Egg-eaters. Oviparous. |
| Dipsadinae | S. and C. America | 60 | No | Dipsas | Arboreal mollusc-eaters. Oviparous. |
| Pareinae | Asia | 16 | No | Pareas | Mollusc-eaters. Oviparous. |
| Xenodermatinae | Asia | ? | No | Xenodermus | Natural history almost unknown. Reproduction apparently unknown. |
| Aparallactinae | Africa | 60 | Yes (front) | Aparallactus | Burrowing. Oviparous. Previously classified with the Viperidae. |

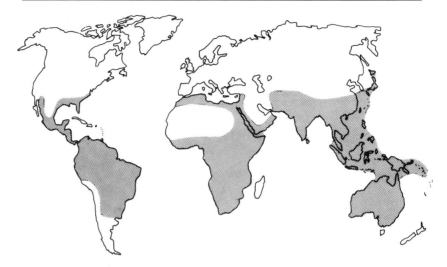

Map 11    Distribution of the Elapidae, excluding sea snakes.

marked with various permutations of red, white or yellow, and black rings, a pattern which may serve to warn or startle predators (Plate 29). They spend most of their lives beneath the surface, in tunnels or beneath rocks and logs etc and most feed on other snakes (especially burrowing kinds), and amphisbaenids. As far as is known, all lay eggs. In temperament, the coral snakes tend to be irascible and unpredictable, thrashing about wildly and biting haphazardly if molested. Despite their small size (the largest grows to little over 1 m, 3 ft) and short fangs, their venom is extremely potent.

In Asia, several other elapids (genera *Maticora* and *Calliophis*) parallel these genera in appearance, activity pattern and diet, and these are also referred to as coral snakes, but they differ from their South American counterparts in being shy and rarely biting. The same is true of the kraits, *Bungarus* species, which inhabit the oriental region and which are also strikingly marked – most are black with white or yellow bands.

The genus *Naja* (Plate 92) contains the species which most epitomise the cobras – fast and graceful snakes which raise the foreparts of their body off the ground and spread their ribs to form a hood when they are disturbed. The genus occurs in Africa and the Middle East (four or five species) and Asia, where the only species, *Naja naja*, is probably the best-known one, with the Indian or spectacled cobra, *Naja naja naja*, a favourite with snake-charmers, and just one of about 10 races of a widely distributed and very adaptable species which grows to about 1.5 m (5 ft) and ranges from western Asia to the Philippines and Taiwan.

Plate 92    The Asian cobra, *Naja naja*, of which many forms are scattered
throughout a large part of Asia.

*Naja haje* is known as the Egyptian cobra, but actually occurs over most of Africa, and may grow to 2.5 m (8 ft), whereas the forest cobra, *Naja melanoleuca* (Plate 50) is slightly longer and is remarkable for the amount of its body which can be raised off the ground – up to 60 per cent of its total length. The latter is a rain forest species but, in general, cobras prefer more open habitats and frequently turn up around farms and villages, doubtless attracted by abundant supplies of their main food in the form of rodents (although birds, their eggs, reptiles, amphibians and fish may also be taken). Most of these cobras are not aggressive, preferring to intimidate their attacker by opening their hood and lunging short of the target, often with a closed mouth. The spitting cobras, however, are a more serious problem. There are three species which fall into this category: *Naja naja sputatrix*, a subspecies of the Indian cobra mentioned above; *Naja nigricollis*, the black-necked cobra from Africa; and *Hemachatus haemachatus*, the ringhals, also from Africa. In these species, the venom ducts, instead of continuing to the tip of each fang, open onto the front, and a stream of venom can be sprayed for some distance. Any which enters the eye of an attacker renders it temporarily blind at the very least, and as a range of 3 m (10 ft) or more can be achieved, this strategy is obviously of great survival value. The Asian form is said to be less proficient than the two African species, but the ringhals is especially feared because, although it grows to only about 1 m (3 ft), it is so easily provoked. This species is also noteworthy for its reproductive habits: it is unique amongst African, Asian and American elapids in giving birth to living young.

The other important group of African elapids are the mambas, *Dendroaspis* species. There are four, of which the largest and most feared is the black mamba, *D. polylepis* (Plate 68), a terrestrial species which can grow to 4 m (13 ft) in length. It is commonly dark grey in colour and its scales have a satiny sheen rather like that of old pewter. The other three mambas are green in colour and arboreal, the most common being the green mamba, *D. angusticeps* (Plate 93) which grows to 2 m (6½ ft) in length. This snake is uniformly green or yellowish green in colour, but the other two species have scales which are edged in black. They are Jameson's mamba, *D. jamesoni*, and the western green mamba, *D. viridis*. Mambas are probably the swiftest of all snakes, especially when travelling through tangled scrub, and they feed on small mammals (especially rodents), reptiles and birds. All are shy and nervous, but they are common and their bites account for several human deaths each year.

Of the remaining African cobras *Boulengerina* are of particular interest because they have adopted a semi-aquatic life-style. The two species are never found far from water and feed entirely on fish. The tree cobras, *Pseudohaje*, both of which are quite rare, are very arboreal and apparently feed mostly on frogs, whereas two genera of garter snakes, *Elaps* and *Elapsoidea* (not to be confused with the harmless North American garter snakes, *Thamnophis*), are small burrowing species.

The king cobra, or hamadryad, *Ophiophagus hannah*, is the largest elapid and the longest venomous snake in the world. It can grow to 5 m (16 ft) and, although it is not common, it has a wide range over India and South-east Asia. It is sometimes found around villages and ruined buildings etc and feeds almost entirely on other snakes. Its venom is very potent and is produced in large quantities.

The Australasian region is very rich in elapids, this being the only part of the world where venomous snakes (all belonging to this family) are in the majority. The largest and most dangerous is the taipan, *Oxyuranus scutellatus*, which reaches almost 3 m (10 ft) in total length and is reputedly very aggressive. Fortunately for Australians, it is restricted to the thinly populated northern part of the country where it appears to be quite rare. Recently, a similar species, the inland taipan, *Oxyuranus microlepidotus*, was recognised. It too is very dangerous but, if anything, is even less common than the taipan. Not so rare, however, are the tiger snakes, *Notechis scutatus* and *N. ater*, two medium-sized snakes marked, as their name suggests, by a number of pale crossbands on a predominantly brown background. They both occur in the southern parts of the continent and *N. ater* is also found in Tasmania and on a number of off-shore islands.

Two Australian species of special interest are the death adders, *Acanthophis antarcticus* and *A. pyrrhus*. Despite their popular names, these are elapids which have departed from the usual, rather conservative, shape of most of the family to become short, stocky, and remarkably viper-like in appearance. Both species inhabit scrubby or desert regions, with *A. antarcticus* being by far the most common and widespread. Both are nocturnal and may remain buried beneath a layer of sand or soil to escape detection during the day. The brown snakes, *Pseudonaja* species, have hoods and are unusual amongst elapids in constricting their prey in addition to envenomating it. The six species cover the entire continent between them. Other genera of large Australian elapids are *Demansia*, whipsnakes (four species), and *Pseudechis*, black snakes (four species).

The remainder of the 60-odd elapids from this region are mostly small, inoffensive burrowing snakes. Many of them are brightly-coloured, such as *Simonelaps australis* (yet another 'coral' snake) and its congeners, and the appropriately named bandy-bandy, *Vermicella annulata*, spectacularly patterned with black and white rings from end to end. As far as is known, most of these diminutive elapids feed on lizards, smaller snakes such as *Typhlina* species and, probably, insects. Most Australian elapids are egg-layers, but a number are ovo-viviparous and one or more species of *Denisonia* appear to be truly viviparous.

The Pacific islands are not without their quota of elapids: New Guinea has a number of species (including the taipan), three species occur on the Solomon Islands, and on Fiji a single species, *Ogmodon vitianus*, is the only venomous snake. It is restricted to Viti Levu island and the occurrence of an advanced snake on so remote an island is difficult to account for.

Plate 93    The green mamba, *Dendroaspis angusticeps*, is an African member of the cobra family.

## Hydrophinae and Laticaudinae – Sea Snakes

The remaining two sub-families of elapids consist of sea snakes. They are sometimes considered as a separate family distinct from the terrestrial elapids, although the characteristics which would appear to set them apart are all adaptations to a marine habitat and are probably of little taxonomic importance: their nostrils can be closed by a valvular arrangement of muscles, as can the lingual fossa (tongue notch), their tails are laterally compressed to become paddle-shaped (Fig. 9) and most lack the enlarged ventral scales which enable terrestrial snakes to move about. They range throughout most of the tropical parts of the Pacific Ocean, from the Cape of Good Hope, through the Indian Ocean, around the Indonesian archipelago to northern Australia and, although most are more or less restricted to coastal waters, one species crosses the Pacific and is found along the west coast of tropical America.

About 35 species are found in the sub-family Hydrophinae, of which 20 or more belong to the genus *Hydrophis*. The widest-ranging species, however, is *Pelamis platurus*, the yellow-bellied sea snake, which can be thought of as a pelagic animal. Much remains to be learnt about the ecology and behaviour of sea snakes, not least of which is the motivation behind the colossal shoals of them which are occasionally sighted. These may be many miles long and invariably consist of a single species. Normally, sea snakes are not aggressive animals and bites from them are rare, but individuals have been known to attack divers, for instance, on odd occasions. All feed on fish, especially eels, although some apparently specialise in fish eggs, and others are known to take marine invertebrates. Due to their totally marine existence, the Hydrophinae are of necessity ovo-viviparous, but the other sub-family of sea snakes, the Laticaudinae, contains four species, in the genus *Laticauda*, which come ashore to lay eggs above the tide-line. Unlike the Hydrophinae, these species do have enlarged ventral scales to enable them to move across the land, as do members of the genera *Aipysurus* (six species) and *Emydocephalus* (one species) although, strangely, these do *not* come ashore to lay their eggs, being ovo-viviparous, and because their relationships with the *Laticauda* species are not fully understood they are only tentatively placed in the same sub-family.

## Viperidae – Vipers

The vipers, Viperidae, are generally reckoned to be the most advanced snakes (although, like just about every aspect of reptile taxonomy, not all experts would agree). There is, however, no disputing the fact that they have evolved the most sophisticated apparatus for killing their prey: long tubular fangs, situated at the front of their mouths and hinged so that they can be folded away when not required. A typical viper is a short thick-set snake with keeled scales and a broad, spade-shaped head (to accommodate its large venom glands). The top of the head is covered with numerous small scales, and the pupil is vertically elliptical. Vipers occur over most of the world, but are absent from the Australasian region, having appeared after this block of land became separated from the main land-mass. Although they occupy just about every possible habitat except the oceans, two niches which they occupy to a far greater extent than other snakes are the world's deserts and mountains. They are especially suited to the latter because their body-shape retains heat efficiently, and the tendency throughout the family to reproduce ovo-viviparously or viviparously bestows special advantages on reptiles living in cool places (see page 67). Thus, vipers are found further north and further south than other snakes, and also at higher altitudes (Map 12).

The family is divided into three distinct sub-families: Azemiopidae; Viperinae; and Crotalinae. The first contains only one species, *Azemiops feae*, Fea's viper, a rare montane species from China, Burma and Tibet. It is distinct from other vipers in having large head shields similiar to those of colubrids and elapids, and in having smooth scales. It is also one of the few oviparous species in the family.

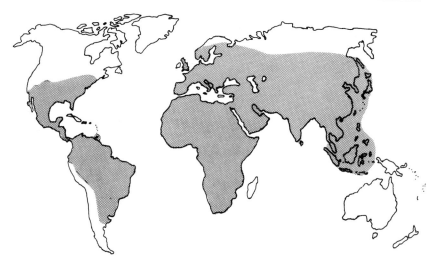

Map 12    Distribution of the Viperidae.

## Viperinae – Typical Vipers

The Viperinae, often known as 'true' vipers, is restricted to the Old World. The type genus, *Vipera*, has several species in Europe, North Africa, the Middle East and Asia. *V. berus*, the adder or northern viper, has an enormous range from western Europe right across to the eastern shores of Asia. In typical *Vipera* fashion, it is a short, stout snake with heavily keeled scales and a dark zig-zag vertebral line (Plate 1). It is unusual amongst snakes in displaying sexual dimorphism, the markings of the male contrasting more strongly than those of the female. The sand viper, *V. ammodytes*, the largest and most dangerous of the European species, inhabits dry, rocky hillsides and has a prominent nasal horn (Plates 20 and 94). Lataste's Viper, *V. latastei*, has an upturned snout rather than a horn, as does *V. aspis*, both species which occur up to moderately high altitudes in the mountains of Spain and central Europe respectively. The meadow viper, *V. ursinii*, is the smallest species and also occurs fairly high up – its fragmented distribution consists of small 'islands' of suitable habitat scattered over an area which is less suitable. It preys largely on insects, especially crickets and grasshoppers, in the absence of more substantial prey.

The remaining members of the genus are somewhat larger and more dangerous than the above species, and include Russell's viper, *Vipera russelli*, found from India to South-east Asia. This infamous species grows to 1.5 m (5 ft) in length and is marked with dark-brown blotches, edged with white, on a lighter ground. It has a well-deserved reputation for

Plate 94    The sand viper, *Vipera ammodytes*, from south-eastern Europe.

being irascible and quick to strike without warning. Several other species are found in the extreme east of Europe and the Middle East, of which *V. lebetina* is unique within the genus, being an egg-layer, although it does this only in the southern parts of its range, conforming to the usual pattern elsewhere.

In Africa, the genus *Bitis* is the most widespread and important genus of vipers. These are mostly heavy-bodied, sluggish snakes with wide heads and very long fangs. The largest, *B. gabonica*, has already been referred to' on account of its disruptive colouration. Its head is flat and wide and the markings along its length, although distinctive and bold, provide near perfect camouflage when it is resting amongst vegetation in broken sunlight (Plate 95). It is a rain forest species and therefore restricted to tropical Africa. A similar but smaller species is *B. nasicornis*, the rhinoceros viper, which is if anything even more extravagantly marked, and which has a pair of prominent horns on the tip of its snout. Its preference for damp habitats provides an alternative common name of 'river Jack'. *B. arietans*, the puff adder, is probably the commonest bitid, and certainly amongst the most feared for its habit of lounging around on tracks after dark, seemingly waiting to be trodden on. This is a snake of more open country than the previous two, as is the berg adder, *B. atropos*, which occurs from sea-level up to 3,000 metres in the Drakensburg Mountains. Three species of *Bitis* are desert dwellers. These are *B. caudalis*, *B. cornuta*, and *B. peringueyi*. The first two are 'horned' vipers, the horns being situated above the eyes, and Peringuey's viper is remarkable in having its eyes positioned on top of its head so that they look almost directly upwards. All these species are adept at shuffling down into the sand, and all 'sidewind'.

Staying in Africa, the genus *Causus* (night adders) is regarded as primitive due to the oviparous habits of its six members, and the arrangement of large scales on their heads. The commonest of these species is *C. rhombeatus*, which occurs throughout Africa south of the Sahara. Like all of the genus, it is nocturnal and feeds on frogs and toads. Night adders have greatly elongated venom glands, although their bite is not regarded as particularly dangerous.

The genus *Echis* contains two species, *E. carinatus* and *E. coloratus*, both known as carpet vipers or saw-scaled vipers. The former is found from West Africa, through western Asia as far as India and Sri Lanka, but it is replaced in the Middle East by *E. coloratus*. Both are small, growing to about 75 cm (30 in), but they are well-camouflaged, bad-tempered and have a potent venom. Coupled to this is a range which covers an area with a high proportion of peasant farmers, an equation which results in many fatalities. The heavily-keeled scales may be rubbed together to produce a buzzing or rasping sound, a warning strategy which is sometimes mimicked by the harmless egg-eating snake, *Dasypeltis scaber*.

North Africa and the Middle East is also the home of a further selection

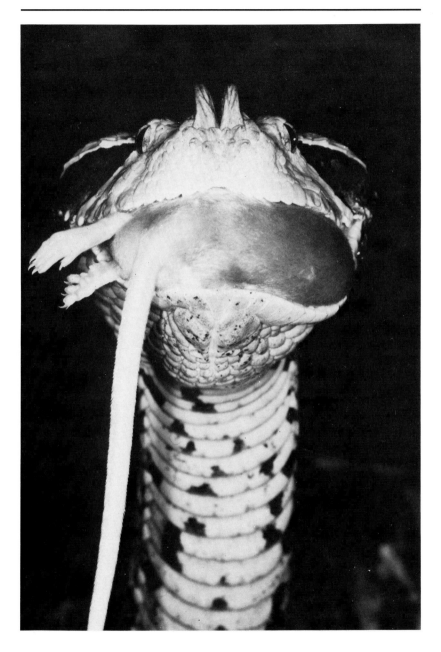

Plate 95    The gaboon viper, *Bitis gabonica*, the largest African viper, swallowing a mouse.

of desert vipers: *Cerastes cerastes*, the desert horned viper (Plate 96), *C. vipera*, the Sahara horned viper, *Pseudocerastes persicus*, the Persian horned viper, and *Eristicophis macmahonii*, McMahon's viper. All are small, to about 80 cm (32 in), and all are well adapted to living in arid conditions, often in loose, shifting sand. They feed on small mammals and lizards and are nocturnal in habit. All are potentially dangerous to man.

The remaining group of viperins contains the only species of vipers to have opted for an arboreal existence. These are the bush vipers, genus *Atheris*, of which about eight species are recognised, all central African. Most are greenish in colour and have prehensile tails, but the most bizarre species is *A. hispida*, the rough-scaled viper, which has heavily-keeled, pointed scales which curl at their apex and give the snake a spiky appearance. *A. superciliaris* was formerly classified within the genus *Bitis* as this, and one other, *A. hindii*, are not arboreal and differ from other *Atheris* species in other ways. Both are rare, and the ecology of all the bush vipers is very poorly known.

## Crotalinae – Pit Vipers

The third, and most widespread, sub-family of the Viperidae is that of the pit vipers, Crotalinae. These snakes differ from other vipers by possessing a unique heat-sensitive organ (the 'pit') between the eye and the nostril

Plate 96   The horned viper, *Cerastes cerastes*, a specialised desert species.

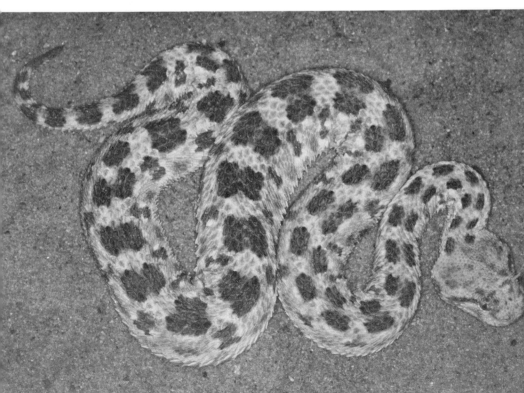

(see also page 33). One genus, *Agkistrodon*, is found in Asia and America, and one, *Trimeresurus*, is restricted to Asia. The other four genera are found only in the New World.

Three species of *Agkistrodon* occur in North and Central America. *A. piscivorus* is known as the cottonmouth owing to its habit of gaping widely to display the white interior of its mouth if it is threatened. It is dark brown in colour with indistinct cross-bars, and it inhabits moist and swampy places where it feeds chiefly on fish and amphibians. The beautifully marked copperhead, *A. contortrix* (Plate 27), is orange and chestnut in colour, and the cantil, or Mexican moccasin, *A. bilineatus*, is rather similar to the cottonmouth in appearance but differs in having thin cream lines on its head.

Ten species of *Agkistrodon* occur in Asia. *A. halys* ranges from Russia (where its distribution includes a small part of Europe), across to Japan. It grows to less than a metre (3 ft) in length and is not very dangerous, but the bite of another species, *A. acutus*, the sharp-nosed pit viper, from South-east Asia, may prove fatal. Another dangerous species, *A. rhodostoma*, from Malaya is the only viper other than Fea's viper to have smooth scales. Most of these Asian pit vipers are terrestrial, inhabiting lowland forests and plantations, but one species, *A. himalayanus*, lives as high as 4,900 m (16,000 ft) in the Himalayas.

The other Old World pit vipers, contained in a single genus, *Trimeresurus*, are arboreal: many are green in colour and have prehensile tails. The thirty-odd species are variously known as bamboo or temple vipers. *T. wagleri*, Wagler's pit viper, is common in South-east Asia and a number live in the Buddhist snake temple on the island of Penang, where they appear to tolerate frequent handling by visitors. *T. popeorum* (Plate 97) grows to almost a metre (3 ft) and is found from the Himalayan foothills to Indonesia. The Indian peninsula is the home of *T. gramineus*, replaced in Sri Lanka by *T. trigonocephalus*. All four of the above snakes are predominantly green in colour, but certain of the less arboreal species, such as *T. purpuromaculatus* are brownish.

In the New World, *Trimeresurus* are paralleled closely by members of the genus *Bothrops*. This enormous genus (nearly 50 species) contains arboreal species as well as several which are terrestrial. Arboreal forms are often referred to collectively as palm vipers, and include *B. schlegelii*, which is also known as the eye-lash viper, an allusion to a patch of bristly scales over each eye. It may be yellow or green in colour and ranges from southern Mexico to northern South America. *B. lichenosus*, from the same general area, is mottled in greys and greens, a pattern which resembles the lichen

Plate 97 (overleaf)   An Asian pit viper, *Trimeresurus popeorum*, an arboreal species which uses its brightly-coloured tail as a lure.

Plate 98  *Bothrops atrox*, a common South American pit viper, sometimes known as
the fer-de-lance.

that covers the trunks and branches of the trees amongst which it lives.
　　More important, from the human point of view, are a number of species
which are dangerous to man. These are cryptically-coloured, terrestrial
species which are easily trodden on when passing through overgrown
places. *B. atrox* (Plate 98) is known as the barba amarilla (yellow beard)
or, erroneously, as the fer-de-lance. This common species, which grows to
about 2 m (6$\frac{1}{2}$ ft), inhabits plantations and forests, especially alongside
streams, and is found from Mexico to Brazil. It almost certainly accounts
for more deaths than any other South American snake. *B. lanceolatus*, the
true fer-de-lance, is restricted to the island of Martinique, and the only
other West Indian species is *B. carribeus* from St Lucia, a handsome snake
blotched with black or brown on a pale brown or cream back ground. Two
other species worth noting are *B. nummifer*, the jumping viper, which, as its
name suggests, strikes so fiercely that its body moves forward, and *B.
ammodytoides*, an Argentinian species which occurs further south than any
other snake.

Plate 99    The pygmy rattlesnake, *Sistrurus miliarius*, a small pit viper.

Central America and the northern parts of South America also form
the range of the largest pit viper, the bushmaster, *Lachesis muta*. This
impressive but rarely-seen snake can grow to 3 m (10 ft) or more and, like
the terrestrial *Bothrops* species from the same part of the world, inhabits
the leaf-strewn rain forest floor. Its scales are strongly keeled and rough
and this has given rise to the name 'mapapire ananas' (pineapple snake)
in some parts of its range. It is yellow or pale brown in colour, with
diamond-shaped blotches of deep brown along its back (Plates 17 and
100). It is the only pit viper in the New World to lay eggs.

The remaining pit vipers belong to two genera of rattlesnakes – *Crotalus*
and *Sistrurus*. These snakes, of which there are about 30 species and numerous
subspecies altogether, must be amongst the most instantly recognisable
of all venomous snakes. Their rattle, the structure of which is described on
page 40, is one of the most bizarre developments amongst the serpents,
though its purpose is still in some doubt. Although rattlesnakes are
popularly associated with the deserts and badlands of North America and

177

Plate 100 The world's largest pit viper, *Lachesis muta*, the bushmaster, at home on the tropical rain forest floor.

Mexico, they are by no means restricted to dry environments.

The three species of *Sistrurus* are known as pygmy rattlesnakes, and consist of the massasauga, *S. catenatus*, which extends from the Mexican border to the Canadian border in eastern North America, *S. miliarius*, (Plate 99), found throughout the south-eastern United States, and *S. ravus*, which occurs in central Mexico. There appears to be a preference for moist, even swampy, habitats amongst the members of this genus, and amphibians, as well as fish, are eaten. Pygmy rattlesnakes are distinguished from other rattlesnakes by having nine large plates covering the tops of their heads instead of numerous small scales.

The majority of the rattlesnakes belong to the genus *Crotalus*, which contains a number of small, fairly innocuous species in addition to the better known large and dangerous ones. The odd one out is *C. catalinensis*, from Santa Catalina island off Baja California. This rare species has only the vestiges of a rattle and is usually referred to by the contradictory, but descriptive, name of 'rattleless rattlesnake'. The most notorious of the North American species are the western diamondback, *C. atrox* (Plate 8), and the eastern diamondback, *C. adamanteus*. Both of these species can exceed 2 m ($6\frac{1}{2}$ ft) in length and, as their names indicate, their markings consist of a series of diamond-shaped dorsal blotches. Other large diamond-backed species include *C. ruber*, the red diamondback of Baja California, and the cascabel, *C. durissus*, a Central American species with a wide range and many geographical variants. Several species are irregularly banded: *C. horridus*, the timber rattlesnake, and *C. viridis*, the prairie rattlesnake, being examples. All of the above, several of which are divided into many subspecies, are large species covering a variety of habitats from deserts to tropical rain forests, and all feed primarily on mammals such as rodents and lagomorphs (rabbits and hares), and birds. There may be a trend towards carrion-feeding amongst several of these species.

In the mountains of the southern United States and northern Mexico are found a group of small (to 1 m, 3 ft) species. These include *C. pricei*, the twin-spotted rattlesnake, *C. willardi*, the ridge-nosed rattlesnake, and *C. lepidus*, the rock rattlesnake. All of these small rattlers are strictly montane in habit and may be found up to 3,000 m (10,000 ft) in mountain ranges such as the Chiricahua and Sierra Madre. They feed on small mammals, birds and lizards.

Although many species occur in arid regions (e.g. *C. scutulatus*, the mojave rattlesnake, *C. tigris*, the tiger rattlesnake, as well as some of those listed above), only one, the sidewinder, *C. cerastes*, shows any obvious signs of adaptation to desert life. This species parallels several of the true vipers of North Africa and the Middle East in its appearance, notably the horns over its eyes, and in its sidewinding method of locomotion, for which it is named. Unlike the Old World species, however, the sidewinder is only mildly venomous and does not pose a serious threat to humans.

All rattlesnakes, as far as is known, give birth to living young. They remain amongst the most fascinating groups of snakes to the layman, and one of the most studied. In particular, Laurence Klauber's monumental work on the natural history of rattlesnakes (all 1,536 pages of it) must rank as one of the most thorough monographs on a group of animals ever published (see Bibliography).

# Bibliography

The following lists of references are intended as a starting point for those wishing to expand their knowledge of snakes, and, as such, are not comprehensive. Where more than one book covers a similar aspect of herpetology I have tried to list the most readable and readily accessible title: unfortunately specialised books quickly go out of print and many of the older works are now difficult to obtain.

## Section 1

Books dealing with snakes or reptiles in general.

Fitch, H.S. (1970), 'Reproductive Cycles of Lizards and Snakes', *Univ. Kansas Mus. Nat. Hist., Misc. publ. No. 52.*

Goin, C.J., Goin, O.B. and Zug, G.R. (1978), *Introduction to Herpetology* (3rd edition), W.H. Freeman and Co., San Francisco.

Heatwole, H (1976), *Reptile Ecology*, University of Queensland Press.

Mattison, C. (1982) *The Care of Reptiles and Amphibians in Captivity*, Blandford Press, Poole, Dorset.

Morris, R. and Morris, D. (1965), *Men and Snakes*, McGraw-Hill, New York.

Parker, H.W. and Grandison, A.G.C. (1977), *Snakes – a natural history*, British Museum (Nat. Hist.) and Cornell University Press, London and Ithaca.

Swaroop, S. and Grab, B. (1954), 'Snakebite Mortality in the World', *Bulletin of the World Health Organisation, X; pp. 35–76.*

## Section 2

Books or articles giving detailed information about a species, group of species, or family of snakes.

Dunson, W.A. (editor) (1975), *The Biology of Sea Snakes*, University Park Press, Baltimore and London.

Fitch, H.S. (1960), 'Autecology of the Copperhead', *Univ. Kansas Pub. Mus. Nat. Hist. 13 (4); 85–288.*

Gans, C. (1976), 'Aspects of the Biology of Uropeltid Snakes', in

*Morphology and Biology of Reptiles* (eds. Bellairs and Cox), Academic Press, London.

Klauber, L.M. (1972), *Rattlesnakes. Their Habits, Life Histories and Influence on Mankind*, 2 volumes (revised edition). University of California Press, Berkeley, Los Angeles and London.

Minton, S.A. and Minton, M.R. (1969 and 1971), *Venomous Reptiles*, Schribner's, New York, and George Allen and Unwin, London.

Phelps, Tony (1981), *Poisonous Snakes*, Blandford Press, Poole, Dorset.

Pope, C.H. (1962), *The Giant Snakes*, Routledge and Kegan Paul, London.

Prestt, I. (1971), 'An ecological study of the viper, *Vipera berus*, in southern England', *J. Zool. London, 165; 373–418.*

## Section 3

Guides to the identification of snakes (and sometimes other reptiles and amphibians) in a particular region. Many of these also include sections on the natural history of snakes which applies not only to those species listed. It will probably be noted that some areas are well covered, others not at all, and books dealing with a small area often give more detailed information than larger surveys.

Arnold, E.N. and Burton, J.A. (1978), *A Field Guide to the Reptiles and Amphibians of Britain and Europe*, William Collins, Sons and Co., Glasgow.

Ashton, R.E. and Ashton, P.S. (1981), *Handbook of Reptiles and Amphibians of Florida, part one: The Snakes*, Windward Publishing Inc., Miami.

Broadley, D.G. and Cock, E.V. (1975), *Snakes of Rhodesia*, Longman Rhodesia (Pvt) Ltd., Salisbury.

Cogger, H.G. (1979), *Reptiles and Amphibians of Australia (revised edition)*, A.H. and A.W. Reed Pty Ltd., Sydney.

Conant, R. (1975), *A Field Guide to Reptiles and Amphibians of Eastern/Central North America* (2nd edition), Houghton Mifflin Co., Boston.

Fitzsimmons, V.F.M. (1962), *Snakes of Southern Africa*, Purnell and Sons (S.A.) (Pty) Ltd., Johannesburg.

Frazer, D. (1983), *Reptiles and Amphibians in England*, William Collins, Sons and Co., Glasgow.

McCoy, M. (1980), *Reptiles of the Solomon Islands*, Wau Institute Handbook No. 7, Papua New Guinea.

Pitman, C.R.S. (1974), *A Guide to the Snakes of Uganda* (revised edition), Wheldon and Wesley, England.

Reitinger, F.F. (1978), *Common Snakes of South East Asia and Hong Kong*, Heinemann, Hong Kong.

Roze, J.A. (1966), *La Taxonomia y Zoogeografia de los Ofidios de Venezuela*, Central University of Venezuela, Caracas.

Stebbins, R.C. (1966), *A Field Guide to Western Reptiles and Amphibians*, Houghton Mifflin Co., Boston.

Tennant, A. (1984), *The Snakes of Texas*, Texas Monthly Press.

Wall, F. (1921), *Ophidia Taprobanica, or the Snakes of Ceylon*, H.R. Cottle, Ceylon.

Wright, A.H. and Wright, A.A. (1957), *Handbook of Snakes of the United States and Canada*, 3 volumes inc. bibliography, Cornell University Press, Ithaca, New York.

## Section 4

Books about snake-hunting and snake-hunters. As well as making enjoyable reading for the armchair herpetologist, these books contain much first-hand information about snakes by people who have spent a large part of their lives studying their habits.

Kauffield, C. (1957), *Snakes and Snake-hunting*, Hanover House, Garden City, New York.

Kauffield, C. (1969), *Snakes: The Keeper and the Kept*, Doubleday and Co. Inc., New York.

Spawls, S. (1979) *Sun, Sand and Snakes*, Collins & Harvill.

Wood, L.N. (1951), *Raymond L. Ditmars*, Robert Hale Ltd., London.

Wykes, A. (1960), *Snake Man – The Story of C.J.P. Ionides*, Hamish Hamilton, London.

## Section 5

Periodicals and journals published by herpetological societies and available to members. Unfortunately the addresses of these societies are not constant and cannot usefully be given here, but libraries, museums, universities and zoological gardens should be able to help. An asterisk denotes publications which cater mainly for the amateur, the others being somewhat more scientifically orientated.

*British Journal of Herpetology* (2 per annum) and *\*British Herpetological Society Bulletin* (2 per annum), published by the British Herpetological Society (BHS).

*\*Herpetofauna* (2 per annum), published jointly by the Australian Herpetological Society and the New Zealand Herpetological Society.

*Herpetologica* (4 per annum), published by the Herpetologists' League (USA).

*\*The Herptile* (4 per annum), published by the International Herpetological Society (UK).

*Journal of Herpetology* (4 per annum) and *\*Herpetological Review* (4 per annum), published by the Society for the Study of Amphibians and Reptiles (SSAR) (USA).

*\*Journal of the Herpetological Association of Africa* (2 per annum), published by the Herpetological Association of Africa (HAA).

*\*Litteratura Serpentarium* (6 per annum), published by the Dutch Snake Society. This excellent publication, which is available in English or Dutch editions, is the only one dealing solely with snakes.

Many other amateur societies exist, especially in North America, all of which produce publications of interest and many of which hold regular meetings – the major societies, listed above, will be able to provide details of these if required.

# Index

Figures in **bold** refer to page numbers of illustrations.